YOU'RE LUCKY YOU'RE FUNNY

ALSO BY PHIL ROSENTHAL

Everybody Loves Raymond: Our Family Album,
with Ray Romano, photographs by Tom Caltabiano

YOU'RE LUCKY YOU'RE FUNNY

How Life Becomes a Sitcom

PHIL ROSENTHAL

VIKING

VIKING
Published by the Penguin Group
Penguin Group (USA) Inc., 375 Hudson Street, New York, New York 10014, U.S.A.
Penguin Group (Canada), 90 Eglinton Avenue East, Suite 700, Toronto, Ontario, Canada M4P 2Y3
(a division of Pearson Penguin Canada Inc.)
Penguin Books Ltd, 80 Strand, London WC2R 0RL, England
Penguin Ireland, 25 St. Stephen's Green, Dublin 2, Ireland (a division of Penguin Books Ltd)
Penguin Books Australia Ltd, 250 Camberwell Road, Camberwell, Victoria 3124, Australia
(a division of Pearson Australia Group Pty Ltd)
Penguin Books India Pvt Ltd, 11 Community Centre, Panchsheel Park, New Delhi – 110 017, India
Penguin Group (NZ), Cnr Airborne and Rosedale Roads, Albany, Auckland 1310, New Zealand
(a division of Pearson New Zealand Ltd)
Penguin Books (South Africa) (Pty) Ltd, 24 Sturdee Avenue, Rosebank, Johannesburg 2196, South Africa

Penguin Books Ltd, Registered Offices: 80 Strand, London WC2R 0RL, England

First published in 2006 by Viking Penguin, a member of Penguin Group (USA) Inc.

1 3 5 7 9 10 8 6 4 2

ISBN 0-670-03799-0

Printed in the United States of America
Set in Minion
Designed by Ginger Legato

During our second season of *Raymond,* I accompanied Ray and Peter Boyle on their trip to New York, where they guest-starred on an episode of *Cosby*. Bill Cosby, one of my (and Ray's) idols, sat us down for a chat during a break in rehearsals. I was thrilled to be there. "I'm not crazy about too many of the sitcoms today," he said. "Seems like some guys just want to get even with their parents." And then he looked at me. It was awkward.

This book is dedicated to my parents, who I got even with long ago, when I decided to make good on my childhood threats to go into show business, and to the rest of my family, especially Ben and Lily, and my sweet and lovely bride, Monica. In spite of what appears to be televised evidence to the contrary, I love these people and thank them for their lifetime of support, worry, and script fodder.

ACKNOWLEDGMENTS

Many thanks to David Vigliano, my trusted book agent, and Rick Kot and all my new friends at Viking Press, my right arm, Erin Champion, and especially Danelle Morton for her interviews and invaluable feedback.

Thanks to every friend and mentor, including the great showrunners and writers of my favorite pastimes, and to everybody I loved working with, in and out of the Writers' Room, on *Everybody Loves Raymond.*

YOU'RE LUCKY YOU'RE FUNNY

PROLOGUE

My brother, Richard, got married on September 5, 1993. I was the best man, and with that honor comes the giving of the toast. I had been earning a living as a writer on an assortment of television sitcoms for about four years at this point, and so I felt there was an expectation to be humorous whenever forced to speak in public—a self-imposed pressure, but real nonetheless, as if I deeply needed to communicate to people, "See, I can be funny, it's not my fault the shows are terrible."

And so I racked my brain for material. Material at family functions often focused on the family at hand, and my particular family had served me well in the past—years earlier I wrote a little poem at my parents' twenty-fifth anniversary party (at their nonstop insistence) that seemed to be hilarious to the relatives and friends. "Better than Broadway!" I had been told. But now, at this wedding, I was thirty-three, and there were people there who didn't know the family, and worse, didn't know me—but here he is: the Hollywood toastmaster. This could be a bad wedding, meaning I could bomb. And then it hit me, an anecdote that had actually happened, that I had suppressed for several years, that drove me nuts then and thinking about it again now rekindled the nuts, and that illustrated the insanity in our family and would serve as a warning to Richard's bride, Karen, as to why she would perhaps reconsider marrying into this psycho ward. Why she should run screaming into the hills rather than subject herself to a life of unrelenting complaining and unbearable frustration, petty domestic politics and life under maternal rule. The more I thought about this story, I realized it wasn't funny at all, but that didn't matter anymore. I had to tell it as a purely cautionary tale. The fact that the toast would come at the wedding reception and that my brother and his wife would be already married didn't change the urgency of my warning.

"Karen," I started. "There is still time to run."

I explained: When I first started to make a little money in Hollywood, I bought my mom, for Hanukkah, a gift of the Fruit-of-the-Month Club.

And then came the phone call from my mother in Rockland County, New York: "Philip, we got the pears."

"Oh, that's good, Ma. You like them?"

"Yes, they're very nice, but please . . . it's an entire box of pears. There must be twelve or fourteen pears here. There're so many pears. Please, Philip, do me a favor. Don't ever send us any more food again, okay?"

I said, "Well, Ma . . . another box is coming next month."

She said, "What? More pears?"

I said, "No, Ma, a different fruit every month."

"EVERY MONTH? My God, Max, he got us in some kind of cult. What am I supposed to do with all this fruit?"

"I don't know," I told her. "Most people like it. You eat it. . . . You share it with your friends."

"Which friends?!"

"I don't know . . . Lee and Stan."

"Lee and Stan buy their own fruit!"

"Oh my God, Ma . . ."

"Why did you do this to me?"

"What is happening?"

"I can't talk anymore, there's too much fruit in the house!"

I went on to describe my father's misery as well at this misfortune that had befallen them. ("You think we're invalids? We can't get our own fruit?") The wedding guests laughed. No one laughed harder than my parents, who really did treat the gift of fruit from their son as if they'd received a box of heads from a murderer. Richard and Karen remain married to this day and have even brought two children into the world.

My warning didn't take. Nobody listens to me. Maybe you will.

I guess if we have to classify this book, it is a memoir of sorts. (That's right, Oprah, and I'll swear it's all true even if you make the mean face at me on the couch.) We'll also, if you're interested, get into how to make a show, specifically the show *Everybody Loves Raymond.* We'll see how it came to be, how "writing what you know" is not just a saying but essential, and how almost anyone's life can be turned into fuel for comedy. We'll use, for example, my life—where I'm from, the other jobs and other shows I toiled on, my relationships with family, with women, with The Writers' Room, with show business, and how all of it found its way into the work, became the work, to the point where it wasn't work anymore. And all of it is here—in the hope that you'll be entertained, and maybe learn a thing or two that could help you in your own career, your life, your diet. You'll learn a little about how to write, cast, edit, direct, run, cater, and, most of all, enjoy the gift of a hit show.

I was crazy lucky to get such a gift, and for nine years, I savored it; I loved it; I was tremendously thankful for it. It would not have occurred to me to return it or leave it or be unhappy with it, let alone complain about the gift to whoever gave it to me that it was all "too much."

You still there, Ma?

1

The Lesson of *Mary Poppins*

When I was a four-year-old boy in the Bronx, I made every adult I knew take me to see the best movie in the world, *Mary Poppins.* I saw it six times in 1964. Not only was it funny, colorful, magical, warm, and charming, but it had great songs and the woman I had decided to marry was starring in it—Julie Andrews. Was I alone in this infatuation? Some of you out there must've felt the same way. I considered myself lucky: four years old, and I had found my wife already. I didn't think, *I know there are problems. She doesn't quite know all about me yet. I live in the Bronx and she's in or above London.* I didn't care. She was smart and pretty, could sing like an angel, was funny in a very dry way, made your toys and junk clean up themselves, had wild medicines and friends who were crazy, man. Mary Poppins was practically perfect in every way, and damn it, that's what I wanted in a woman. This wonderment I was getting from the screen, these laughs, this joy . . . got in deep.

Why? Because the movie was a look at a magical gentile life? It wasn't just that, and it's not just a romp—it's not just lighthearted, just dance around and "Fly a Kite." The kite flying *meant* something. And if you've had the great pleasure of watching it with your kids recently, you'll appreciate that this film, unlike almost everything else out there now, is about something. There's a point to it. There's a point to the magic and the fun—there's something underneath—and it's something that stays with you when the two hours are over, that you can integrate into your life. You don't get it consciously when you're four, but the reason you have to see it six times is because this deceptively simple entertainment has been sophisticatedly designed to impart its themes: Kindness. Love your family. Feed the birds. Enjoy your life. Find a wife like Mary. It's not a lesson, just a strong point of view that comes through while you're enjoying yourself.

This was the value system embedded in the screenplay by its authors, Bill Walsh and Don DaGradi, based on the books by P. L. Travers. It's in the best popular entertainment, and it's in everything that has helped make life worth living for me, not just because the movies and shows I loved gave me a way of looking at and understanding the world, but also because they didn't announce themselves as intending to do that. Watching *Mary Poppins* was just the most fun I had ever had in my whole life. When I was four.

And that fun, I soon discovered, was available on the black-and-white television in our apartment, too: *The Honeymooners* and *The Dick Van Dyke Show* ("Hey, wasn't he . . . ?"), and later, shows like *Mary Tyler Moore, Taxi, All in the Family, The Odd Couple, The Cosby Show, Roseanne,* and *The Simpsons.*

I watched too much TV as a kid, and I still do as what passes for an adult today. My parents used to tell me, "Turn that goddamned thing off! What are you going to do, get a job watching television?"

They were right, of course. A life of living is better than a life of watching—except for the fact that I felt that what I was watching was better than what I was living.

I'm a first-generation American. My parents both survived the

Holocaust—my father got out of Germany right after Kristallnacht, but my mother was in a camp. I never met my grandfather Philipp Auerbach—he survived Auschwitz, the death march, and Buchenwald to stay in Germany rather than join his wife and daughter here, and started what came to be known as the Restitution Program, which forced the German government to pay monthly checks to Jews whose businesses were stolen. (The program continues to this day.) Later my folks met in Washington Heights, on the northern end of Manhattan. So many German Jews wound up there, it was nicknamed "Frankfurt on the Hudson." Dad worked in the Garment Center downtown; Mom was a trained paralegal who quit her job to raise my younger brother and me until we both drove her so insane that she had to start working again when I was nine, or go to jail for killing us. So my life was a paradise compared to what those before me went through.

The problem with kids, though, is that they don't care what those before them went through. They just want candy and a bike and a color TV.

I was born in Queens in 1960, we moved to the Bronx when I was two, and in 1968 we moved to "the country," Rockland County, New York, about a half hour upstate from the city. We had a nice little house on a typical suburban street with trees and yards in a typical neighborhood, where every house had the same layout. Only the exteriors distinguished them—some were painted differently, some people with money had a back porch, and the really wealthy folks had a skylight. Mostly nice, typical neighbors with a handful of typical anti-Semites mixed in to keep you on your toes. I had a few good friends but I didn't go out much, mainly because the other kids who weren't my good friends would punch me in the head. I got roughed up all the time by neighbors, kids who lived only two houses down. A bunch of them would ring the doorbell and ask my mother if I could come out and play. My mother, delighted to have an excuse to make me stop watching television, would usher me out the door. And so I'd walk past her, afraid to speak up, into the waiting fists of my enemies. Why didn't I say, "Hey, Mom, these guys don't really want to play with me, they want to punch me in the head"? Because she wouldn't have believed me. That wouldn't happen here in America. And even if she had believed me, at least I was going outside.

I found television to be safer.

I certainly didn't want to fight, as I never saw the point of that. I'm very sensitive, I guess. They always told me I was too sensitive, or a "little wuss." But the sensitivity is important in the other areas of your life, as it's what people respond to in writing or art. The "too much sensitivity" is only bad for the person feeling it.

What was wrong with Philip? I was a very nice kid, according to my mother, "unless you ask him to do something." My mother sent me to child psychologists my entire childhood, starting as early as eight years old. And they all said the same thing: "It's the mother." When she heard that, she would decide, well, that shrink was obviously an idiot, and I'd be sent to another one. It didn't take me long to figure out what to say to the psychologist to get him to say, "It's the mother."

I was thinking about my childhood memories of TV and I remember a drawing I made in second grade of Ralph and Norton that featured a balloon of what they were saying, a particular gag I liked. In retrospect I don't remember having seen it on *The Honeymooners,* which started as a sketch on *The Jackie Gleason Show* (1952–1957), so it must have been from a sketch they did on *The Jackie Gleason Show* later, the one from Miami Beach in the sixties, when I could watch it on Saturday nights. In my drawing, Ralph says to Norton, "You looking for a fat lip?" and Norton says, "If I was looking for a fat anything I'd know where to find it."

So I'm six, seven years old, and this is hilarious to me, *hilarious,* and I'm so taken with it that in school I'm writing it down, probably instead of math.

And I remember, very distinctly, wanting to be Art Carney. At that age you don't know there's writing, you don't know there's directing or producing. You just think, *Art Carney is funny. I'll be him.* People love him. I love him. He's on television.

I also wanted to be an astronaut. I was six years old in 1966 and I did my part for the U.S. space program by being obsessed with it. And then I realized—and I remember coming to this realization pretty early on—that, you know, astronaut, that's a little dangerous. If I was completely honest, the thing I think I liked the most about being one of the astronauts was that they got to be on *Ed Sullivan.*

I understood that by being Art Carney I could have the best part of being an astronaut without the dangerous sit-on-the-rocket-that-may-blow-up part. Going on the *Ed Sullivan Show* was safer. Unless you were the lion tamer, and that fellow, like the astronaut, certainly was not Jewish.

So that's what I loved. I loved *The Jackie Gleason Show,* the variety one, with the opening credits flying in low, skimming the water of Miami Beach, where they had the greatest audience in the world.

And then Jackie Gleason and Art Carney would do the characters, and I imitated them. And I was pretty good. I got laughs at age six around the table, staying up till ten o'clock with my parents' friends while they smoked and had cake.

My parents had, and still have, a very good sense of humor, considering. My father did some tummling in the Catskills and has a hilarious, expressive face and drop-dead timing. But my mother's mother, Oma (German for "Grandma"), whose story, like Philipp's, is the stuff of Important Historical Movies, may have been the funniest. We can trace the roots of the family philosophy back to her. Here's a little example: One day I was visiting Oma, who was now a tiny little bent old lady. She was the Merlin of Matzo Balls, creating these wonders in her thimble of a Washington Heights apartment. I noticed she had new shoes on.

"Those are new shoes, Oma?"

"Yah," she says, wiping a crinkly hand across her white hair.

"They're very nice," I say. "They look comfortable."

"Yah," says Oma wearily. "They're almost *too* comfortable."

This is our family. The body at rest . . . complains.

Later, when we would go to visit Oma in the nursing home, Palisades Gardens, there was a communal dining hall, not unlike a school cafeteria. One day we found her there, eating with the other nice ladies. Oma says, "Look down there, see Mrs. Gruenenbaum?" We saw a little old woman at the end of the table, stuffing plastic forks and knives, napkins, toast, and sugar packets into her purse. She lived at the place, yet she would still take this stuff every day. Oma leans into us, points to Mrs. Gruenenbaum's purse, and says, "If I'm ever missing, look in there."

Gotta love Oma. On her headstone, it should read HERE LIES OMA: A LITTLE TOO COMFORTABLE.

When we're young, we try to be an amalgam of our influences. I was trying to be my mom and dad (who you might think are funny from watching *Raymond*). I was trying to be Jackie and Art; Bill Cosby, Mel Brooks, Woody Allen, and Don Rickles; Walter Matthau, Jack Benny, and all of Jackie's and Carol's and Johnny's other funny guests, and the actors and writers of those great sitcoms I mentioned, and of the great movie comedies, too. You try to be all these other people, and at some point you taste the soup and it's you.

So in junior high school, and especially in Horrible Hebrew School, I became the comedian. I didn't get beat up quite as much, if I could imitate the sketch from Monty Python that had been on the night before. And soon I found an outlet for this in the school plays, and I started getting laughs on stage.

My friend from birth, Stu Goodman, had a father who did not have a sense of humor. He was the one person among my parents' friends I couldn't get a laugh out of. (We think he was in the CIA.)

One day when I was sixteen, he took us to the movies to see something called *Ten from Your Show of Shows,* a collection of ten sketches from a famous TV show from the fifties. Stan Goodman wanted me to see this Sid Caesar person because, to him, I really didn't know what funny was, I just ran around like a monkey's ass. Well, if you can rent that video, or any collection of sketches from *Your Show of Shows,* put this book down and go rent it now. The last sketch in the film is "This Is Your Story," a parody of *This Is Your Life,* and when I saw it, I actually fell out of the chair in the theater. This is widely and correctly regarded by people who were there, by people who weren't there, by blind and deaf people, as the funniest sketch ever written. I won't ruin it here for you. Go, watch it, come back.

Stan Goodman changed my life. I don't think I've ever laughed as hard at any piece of entertainment before or since. It has everything you could want out of life—laughs and more laughs, and at the center of it, without your even realizing it because you're busy crying from the laughing, it's about love.

The next year our high school did a play as a vehicle for me called *Little Me.* It was written by Neil Simon for Sid Caesar on Broadway. Sid Caesar played seven different roles, and I got to play all seven, too. I got to be Sid Caesar. The papers wrote about me, and I became a minicelebrity in high school. We still have the review somewhere, but the joy of discovery, of rehearsing comedy, feeling good at it, and then getting big laughs on a stage from hundreds of parents and kids who would normally be punching me in the head, this was enough to make me understand *Oh, I should be doing this* and *Oh, this is how one gets girls.*

And for me, that was the only way. That was the only way, and that's so typical I apologize for its dullness, because I really was a shrimpy little nothing. I was kind of short and comically skinny. I had a big nose—I looked like one of those birds you buy at Spencer Gifts in the mall that you tip over, and the weight of its beak keeps it tipping into the glass.

When I was seventeen I had a lot of trouble with women, mainly because I had a very screwed-up view of women, view of life, sense of self, haircut—I wish I could go back. You know how you wish you could go back and play everything differently? Because I was such a schmuck, watching TV all the time. See, I think this was the problem: When I was thirteen, for my bar mitzvah, one of my uncles or somebody gave me a three-year subscription to *Playboy.* It may even have been my parents who got me the subscription. I think my mother prided herself on being liberal, and she would say, "There's nothing wrong with it. It's the human body." One day, she's in my room cleaning up in her housecoat with the flowers on it, and she opens up a *Playboy* in front of me to just check it out and says, "Oh, that's not necessary." To a fourteen-year-old boy, "Actually, Ma, that's the most necessary part, yeah."

But what a subscription to a magazine like that does to a kid is totally screw up his view of what women should be, and what they are really, and what his expectations should be. So this is who I'm going after at Clarkstown High School North: the Women of *Playboy.* And I'm a little nebbishy boy who wishes his hair was straight (like the sport-jacketed Men of *Playboy*), so I try blow-drying and parting it but wind up looking like a lopsided tumbleweed on a stick. I'm pining after the most beautiful girls in school because they're like the girls that are idealized in the magazines. I wouldn't approach them; I was too scared. I was going to wait for them to approach me. I would wait to be in the school play. And not just be in the school play, but to have a big part. The fifteen-year-old girls were attracted to that. (By the way, first of all, any straight guy who goes into the theater department can get girls. Very smart to do that, if you're fifteen and reading this. And listen, if you're fifteen and reading this, you're going to need *something* to get girls.)

But even when I did get to be a big star, still, I was terrified of talking to girls. If I could only go back and yell at that kid: "Schmuck, look, look . . . the girls of *Cue 'n' Curtain* are pushovers." But I was scared to death. What if they said yes? *Playboy* magazine talked about all that stuff that you could dream about, which meant the girls were going to expect me to do that. I didn't know how to do that. I didn't know what to do at all. I'm still not so sure. So I was very shy. It was so much easier just to watch television.

And then somehow I got a beautiful girlfriend, beautiful, beautiful—too beautiful. Jody Saposnik. We didn't have that much in common, Jody and I, except for one thing: We both thought she was beautiful. But, of course, this was my second great love (after Julie Andrews), and it also never worked out. Jody Saposnik broke my heart, and I just couldn't get over it. I was obsessed with asking myself, *Why, why would she leave me? I'm nice and funny, why?*

So I'm about seventeen, and *Annie Hall* comes out.

I'm watching *Annie Hall,* and it hits me like a bat to the head. Everyone is leaving the theater laughing and I'm depressed—*This is me, this is me, and I'll never find anybody, I don't want to belong to a club that would have me for a member, this is me.* And after months of this, I remember my mother, yelling, in the housecoat with the flowers, "Would you snap out of it?!" She was seeing a life of loneliness and desolation ahead for her son, screaming at me, "You're not Woody Allen!!" meaning, "You're cuter than him!!" And I'm sitting there thinking, *She doesn't get it. All I want to be is him.* What made it worse was that I realized that I had all the bad parts of him without any of the great parts.

I didn't have another girlfriend for three years after that. Those are prime years of life. It was like being in jail for that time. I wasn't one of those guys that goes, "Got to just get back out there." I was the guy who said, "See what happens when you go out there?"

At least I had my boxy black-and-white friend. I had to wait for color in my life till senior year in high school, when my parents made a deal that if I went to summer school and got an A and a B in geometry and chemistry, instead of the D and the E I had scored on the first go-round, the family would not only get a color television, but this new, really cool thing called cable with the uncut, uncensored movies on HBO.

I got the A and the B. Then I spent months of prime teenage time locked in the den with a sign on the door: PLEASE BE QUIET AND DON'T COME IN. TAPING. "Taping" meant sitting close to the television with a Panasonic audiocassette recorder, holding a microphone to the speaker while *Annie Hall* was on. My father—picture Peter Boyle with glasses and a Jewish accent—would knock on the door: "Are you finished taping?"

"What?! Don't you see the sign? Quiet! It's ruined now! What are you doing?!"

"I'd like to use the bathroom there."

"Use the bathroom in your room!"

"Your mother's in there. She takes a long time."

"I have to do this over now! I got up to the lobster scene! I have to start all over next time!"

"What is this picture, *Annie Hall*? You saw that already."

"Okay, Dad. Just—go to the bathroom."

"I don't get him at all. Why is this funny?"

He couldn't understand. What the hell was I doing? I saw that picture already. I needed to tape it, too? Why? My parents' attitude toward me and my teenage obsessions could still be summed up in two words: Go outside.

Senior year of high school—other kids were drinking, driving, "dating"—I'd go to sleep listening to my tape of *Annie Hall.* Or sneakily stay up late to watch Johnny Carson. I'm not saying that's what led to my success. I'm saying, very clearly, "pathetic." I regret not having lived more, but this was where I was comfortable. Maybe a little too comfortable.

My mother hated to see me sitting there. She once bought me a bottle of booze and told me to go out on New Year's Eve. My parents went out. Steven Goldenberg and I stayed home and watched uncut movies and nightclub comedy on HBO all night while drinking that bottle of Amaretto. Later, my mother was actually proud of me for throwing up like a regular teenager.

I went back to watching television. And movies. Watching *Jaws* at fifteen was a knockout. Leaving the theater with my friends, in that adrenaline rush, with the shocks and the huge laughs, and the visceral power of that thing roaring through me—I'll never forget that. I saw *Jaws* a few times that summer, and I didn't just watch the movie. I'd sit in the front row and turn around, peeking over the top of my seat to watch the audience as that shark's head leaped up out of the water. People literally jumping out of their seats, popcorn flying. What a show. And I'm learning. Timing, editing, directing, acting—I'd watch the audience, watch how they would start to lean forward at the same time, laugh at the same time. The movie was doing that to them. And to the next audience. And all over the world. I saw the power the medium could have. I would tell my folks, "I'm not just watching, I'm learning." They, of course, thought this was complete and utter bullshit. Even I knew it sounded like bullshit as I was saying it . . . but I really *was* learning. Things definitely got through. It's nice to find out later in life that you weren't completely full of shit. Thank God. I'd hate to think I was just wasting my time not being with ladies.

Jaws is not just a roller coaster. There's something more. There's a fable, an adventure, a great comedy—and, you care about the characters. There's a heart inside the thrill ride that makes the thrills better.

Let's go back to Ralph and Norton for a second: The way Norton spoke, the way he moved—everything about him was funny, and you loved him. I always tell this story when I'm trying to emphasize the need for dramatic moments in your sitcom, because if nothing else it grounds the people as people. Because nobody's just ha-ha funny all the time; our lives aren't like that. And by the way, it also makes the next moment funnier, because you believe that the behavior is coming from a real person. There's a moment in *The Honeymooners* that sums this up for me. Do you remember the episode where Norton gets hurt in the sewer?

Ralph and Norton have had a terrible fight and they've ended their friendship. Ralph has thrown him out of the house. You know, "You've been a dope for the last time! Get out! Bah!" And what's funny is that Ralph replaces Norton with somebody exactly like Norton. The guy raids Ralph's fridge the same way, and moves and even dresses like Norton. They're about to go bowling together—then there's a knock at the door. A man runs in and says, "Did you hear about Norton?"

"What?"

"There was an explosion. He was hurt, was hurt in the sewer."

And that moment, that had never happened on *The Honeymooners,* ever, something serious like this. I remember as a little kid being absolutely rocked back, and if I thought about it enough I could cry even now. But Ralph says, "That's my fault that he was there tonight. If anything ever happened to Norton—if anything ever happened to him I'd never forgive myself. I got to get down there." And the new friend says, "You just got done telling me how much you hate him." And Ralph suddenly gets so mad he grabs the guy by the shirt and he tells him, "What I say about Norton is one thing. How I feel about him is another."

And he runs down to the hospital.

That's what grounds everything. It was unsaid, the feeling between Ralph and Norton. You knew they were brothers. As mad as Ralph got at Norton, you knew he loved him. He had to; he was his best friend. He shared everything with him. He was always, "Ha-ha, let's have a drink." "Pour away, mine host!" They were schemers together, they were partners, and to have it expressed in this moment like that . . .

And of course Ralph goes to the hospital and he's going to give a transfusion for Norton. They put him in the gown, and he's fat and he's on his back getting wheeled into the transfusion room as Norton walks out perfectly fine. "Hey, Ralph." "Hey, Norton," as they pass, and then a second later Ralph comes out in his gown, "Bah! What are you doin' here?!" Norton goes, "I'm fine. The sewer cap just landed on my head." And the doctor says, "Mr. Kramden, we're ready for the transfusion now." So Ralph turns slowly to give somebody else, a stranger, a transfusion. Norton tears up when he realizes Ralph was here for him. "You would do that for me? You're the greatest buddy in the world."

That's a beautiful thing. I didn't get along with my brother when we were kids. He was five years younger, and before Richard made his entrance, it was just me, my mom, dad, me, and some more me. And here comes Richard the Cute, with his blond hair and normal nose. We're best friends now, but I would come home from a day of getting picked on and take it out on him. Probably the biggest regret in my life is that there were times when I was not a nice brother. He would beat me at Ping-Pong, and I would punch him, because he was the only one I was bigger than.

I'm sorry, Richard. Maybe that's why I cry at Ralph and Norton. But we all have our own personal connection to the great moments in the shows we love. That's why they become our favorites.

"What I say is one thing, how I feel is another."

Sitting alone by the television, that got through to me. The values underneath got through. They don't really teach values in school.

We look to movies, TV shows, books, music, all the arts to express the things that are truly important to us, or that we have trouble with in real life, and maybe . . . those are the same things. Kindness. Love your family (no matter how crazy). Enjoy your life. Those are the values that we have carried through from every show and movie that we laugh and cry with, right? And the great ones all have something else in common: While you're laughing or crying or jumping at the story, the message they really want to get to you is coming through; the great ones say it without saying it.

You give a transfusion.

You kill the shark that just ate your friend.

You try to catch the lobsters on the floor together.

You fly a kite with your kids.

Personally, I've never done any of those things. I tried the kite thing once with my kids—first attempt, the wind took the kite and smashed it at a bad angle against the ground, snapping the main stick. End of kite. End of family fun. Lots of crying and screaming that Daddy bought a bad kite. But at least sometimes, in our entertainment, in the arts we look for escape in, life works out a little better.

2

We Teach Success

College. Hofstra University, Long Island, New York. 1977–1981. First time away from home. I had never even been to sleepaway camp, had never spent more than a couple of nights out of the house, had never had garlic or food with any flavor.

Mom was not Julia Child. She was, and still is, bright, funny, and supportive, but her kitchen specialties were dry, chewy meats of the "You're not leaving this table until you swallow that" variety. For Passover once, Mom made a recipe she found in a book, Matzo Lasagna. Yes. Instead of noodles, sheets of matzo. The author of this cookbook was clearly an anti-Semite. We gave some Matzo Lasagna to the cat. The cat looked at us, left the house, walked in front of a car.

College. I was a theater major, and from the first day, the school did a very good job of telling all of us very bright-eyed and enthusiastic young actors, "You're never going to make it." I think this was a mandate from the parents who were spending all their money on tuition: "Make them change their majors." So they told us the staggering statistics, and the head of the Drama Department came in and in his first address to us, announced, "Theater is dead."

I was stunned by this attitude. You can't tell me that. I lived for this. I was taking the bus alone at fifteen from Rockland into Port Authority, Times Square (and this was before Disney moved into Times Square), to wait on line at the TKTS booth for half-price Broadway show tickets. I'd have lunch at the seedy Forty-third Street Nathan's, with the communal sauerkraut (still better than eating at home), see a show, and take the bus home—an hour and a half each way. I could tell you why *Pacific Overtures* was a better show than *A Chorus Line.* And then you could tell me why I didn't have a girlfriend.

So let them try to discourage me with facts and figures such as, "There are forty thousand actors in New York City and three jobs." When you're a kid, hearing that doesn't mean anything to you. Every kid in that theater department thinks, *I'll be one of the three.* The professors keep saying, as do the parents, "You'll need something to fall back on." And we answer, "I won't need something to fall back on." And the school shrugs and says, "Okay."

Why do they do that? You can't listen to the kids. We're idiots! You've got to teach us a usable skill! Bartending, Waitering for Beginners, Typing, Shoplifting. We graduated with BFA degrees, for Chrissakes. None of us of any use to society whatsoever.

"Want to see my monologue?"

"Get the hell away from me" is the usual and appropriate response.

Four years and thousands and thousands of dollars, and all we get is a slight warning: "Have something to fall back on." It's a scam, college.

But the girls . . . there were lots of girls who were living alone there. And I'm trying to sell books here, so I'm going to tell you about all the action I got.

All right, shut up.

You should know from the cover, this is not that kind of book. You know what? I want to jump ahead a few years:

Speech for Hofstra Alumni Awards Dinner—October 30, 1999

Thank you, ladies and gentlemen, distinguished faculty members, alumni, and especially my fellow honorees. It is indeed a great pleasure to be in your company . . . and to be the dumbest among you.

Before I continue, I have a confession to make. This might make you want to reconsider giving me such a generous award. I don't know how to tell you this. In the few years I was in residence here in Tower E, I had a toaster oven in my room. Yes, I'm ashamed. While the other students were dutifully smoking hashish, or having relations at all hours of the day, I was making tuna melts.

Which brings me to this—the reason I could not live without my secret toaster oven here at Hofstra. You see, I was on the meal plan. And don't think the irony of a one-hundred-dollar-a-plate dinner in the student center is lost on me, either. There was a time, right here in the student center, when I would have gladly paid someone one hundred dollars to have my tongue removed.

But seriously, back to the toaster oven. I don't want you, President Shuart, to think I was just in my dorm room, flagrantly whipping up hot dogs and reheating Chicken McNuggets like some hoodlum. I was hungry. I was on the meal plan.

More important, though, I was a theater major. And when people would ask me, "How did Hofstra University prepare you for the real world?" I would smile at them and say, "A bachelor of fine arts degree in theater is just what every young man in this country needs on his résumé to get ahead. It's dog-eat-dog out there. I know. I was on the meal plan." And then I would say, "Excuse me, I need to get back to work. Hey shoe shine! Who wants a shine?"

I'd like to tell you all now about the lowest point in my life. After graduation, I had very little money. I was living in the city. I had lost my job as shoe shine boy at Penn Station because most customers were not really interested in hearing one up-tempo and one ballad from a starving waif rubbing their feet. They just want the shine. So I hadn't eaten all day, my bank account was "unavailable," but at least I had a can of tuna fish waiting for me when I got home. I took the A train to my studio apartment in Spanish Harlem at 139th Street and Homicide that I shared with nine other theater majors, and I opened the cupboard to discover that one of my roommates had given my tuna fish to his cat. I went to bed without dinner that night, ladies and gentlemen. I called it bed. You'd call it a torn sleeping bag with two other guys in it. But before I went to bed that night, I opened a newspaper. And I saw a beautiful, big, full-page advertisement. . . . "Hofstra University. We Teach Success."

Huh, I said to myself. *I must've been out that day.*

All right, yes, we know I wasn't out that day. I can't ever say that Hofstra didn't prepare me for life. Better than that, it prepared me for a life I love, and that I'm very lucky to have. Many of the values I employ every day in the running and execution of the TV show, I learned in the theater department here. And I want to mention a few of my professors who made a difference in my life: Doctor Mason, Professor Siegmund, Doctor Tulin. And Mrs. Aden, who taught me how to project, so I can yell at the actors in Los Angeles. I had a chance yesterday to go back on campus and speak to the students, and that was a great joy for me. I'll gladly come back and do that again anytime if you'd like—you don't even have to give me an award. I have some very fond memories of college, the meal plan notwithstanding, and I thank you for the opportunity to return here in such grand style, so I could thank you all in person. And the food has improved.

Okay, I didn't really shine shoes, but I did have some very lousy jobs, which we'll touch on a little later. All grist for the mill. I did actually lose a night's dinner to my roommate's cat once—that's quite a feeling, to be hungry and looking forward to a tuna sandwich and come home to see a cat eating it. I did go to bed hungry that night. I would've eaten Matzo Lasagna. Or the cat.

I don't want you to think I didn't have any luck with girls at Hofstra, either. Once I got cast in plays, with bigger parts junior and senior years, my confidence was back up to where I was ready to get the heart caved in a couple of more times. I threw a season or two of summer stock in there, too, just to make sure I could get humiliated by women outside the tristate area.

I didn't realize it at the time, but summer stock was a fantastic place to learn how to work in episodic television. The schedule was just as crazy. At my favorite place, the New London Barn Playhouse in New Hampshire, we did twelve shows in twelve weeks. One of my best friends from Hofstra, Tom McGowan, a great actor—you know him as Bernie on *Raymond* and Kenny on *Frasier*—got cast with me at New London the same year. So one week we'd be in *Dracula*, the next week a full-blown production of *The Unsinkable Molly Brown*, the next week *California Suite*, and then *Our Town*, *Pal Joey*, and so on. How do you do it? You're nineteen, and there's nothing you'd rather do in your whole life. You know what we got paid? Nothing. Room (ten guys in a barracks in bunk beds) and board (I remember that every Friday there was something called "ham salad").

That was it. It was hot, there were mosquitoes like the plague, and you were far away from home. People actually approached me after a show once and said, "We've never seen a Jew before." I loved summer stock.

Okay, so what really happened to me upon graduating from Hofstra University with a bachelor of fine arts degree? First thing I wanted to do was move to New York City. I had been building toward this my whole life, and here it was. Some of my classmates knew how to find inexpensive places to live, maybe with some friends, find jobs, and start auditioning. I went at it slightly differently. I thought I could really save a lot of money and have it even easier by moving in with my grandmother in Washington Heights. And not with Oma (my mother's mother), but with Crazy Oma (my father's mother), who lived twenty blocks south, 172nd and Broadway. It was a much worse neighborhood, but Crazy Oma had a huge apartment. Seven rooms. I thought I could go days without seeing her. I thought she wouldn't bother me. I thought this was a good idea.

I've said that my mother is the inspiration for Marie, and to a certain extent, she is. Certain character traits, a couple of blind spots, and several plot points have been lifted from my mother's life. But the really crazy part of Marie, maybe even the slightly evil, mean-to-your-daughter-in-law, off-the-charts-manipulative side of Marie, that's Crazy Oma.

First of all, I got what I deserved. A twenty-one-year-old guy does not move into his eighty-year-old German grandma's apartment and expect to get along with her, especially while she's alive.

"Who vas zat boy who came over yesterday?" she yelled at me, day two.

"That was a friend of mine from school, Crazy Oma."

"He had liquor."

"It's Amaretto. It was a gift, you know? Welcome to New York."

"I don't like zat boy. He doesn't come in here anymore."

"What are you talking about? He's my friend. I'm going to have friends here."

"Not him. Not de boy wit de liquor."

"He's not 'the boy with the liquor.' He's very nice."

"Is he a Yewish boy?"

"I'm not marrying him, Oma. He's a friend. Friend."

Crazy Oma didn't have friends. But she had me now.

"Sit down for dinner."

"Um, actually, I'm going out."

"*Nein.* It's dark outside. You don't vant to go out dere. Stay mit me. I got nice meat from Bloch und Falk. Sit down, Philipchen."

My brother still calls me Philipchen when he wants to be extra annoying.

"I won't be home late, I'm meeting friends for dinner downtown."

"Who?"

"Friends. My friends."

"Dat boy wit de liquor?"

It got worse from there. Every move I made, every sound, everything I wore, was under scrutiny from this little-known division of the FBI.

"Look at your hair. Your hair should have a part in it like zat nice Glen Campbell."

I realized . . . I may have made a mistake. I would have to move out as soon as possible, or murder Crazy Oma, sell her body to Bloch und Falk, and keep the seven-room apartment for myself. By the way, in 1981, that was a one-hundred-eighty-five-dollar-a-month rent-controlled apartment.

Crazy Oma won. Two weeks after moving in, I moved out. Lived uptown, near regular Oma, with another friend from school. (Don't worry, not the boy with the liquor.) Washington Heights above 181st Street and west of Broadway is great: cheap rents, nice neighborhood, and a fifteen-minute A train express to midtown. I lived there for eight years.

And what job is a theater major going to get with all those skills acquired from the fancy university? Looked in the paper . . . can't do that or that . . . what's this? "Phone sales." Some of my friends from school and I went down to one of these boiler rooms, and they gave us a book that contained various scripts. So, okay. It's like an acting job, right? Not only that, I was in the television business.

"Congratulations, you've won a television!" was the first line.

We were actually selling farm and implement cleaner. I would go through the script, a lump in my throat, and if I got down to a certain hook without getting hung up on, one of the head guys would come over, pick up another extension on the phone, listen in, and then speak into my ear—and I was just supposed to repeat what he was saying into the phone. I had to be empty from my ear to my mouth. It was nerve-racking. I was cold-calling people like in *Glengarry Glen Ross.* One friend lasted four hours. Tom McGowan lasted four days. For some reason I lasted four weeks; I actually made a couple of sales. I worked forty hours a week and maybe got a hundred dollars a week.

After a while, I'd pray for people to not be home. I felt my soul draining out as I got this first taste of real life.

I would call Kansas and ask, "Is a Mr. Horace Munson there?" and a nice old lady would say, "Just a minute." And then I hear *clop, clop, clop, clop, clop, clop* across a kitchen floor . . . then a screen door creaks open . . .

"Horace . . . telephone . . ."

And way, way in the distance, I hear a tractor shut down . . . and I'm agonizing. "Oh no, don't get off your tractor for this."

And a long, long pause. And the screen door. And *clop, clop, clop, clop.* And an out-of-breath voice from the heartland says, "Hello."

"Congratulations. You've won a television!"

"Aw, shit." And he hangs up.

I'm feeling dirty again just writing this. Sometimes I would call, and the person had died and the woman would start crying just at the mention of his name. And if I was having a good day at the office, it meant I was ripping these people off.

"Congratulations. You've won a television!" Well of course you haven't won a television. You will get a bad television set if you buy $500 worth of crap. It was obscene.

I would feel terrible, but I was unprepared for life. I had wasted it, watching *The Honeymooners* and dancing around the stage like a monkey's ass. In the real world it was hard to get auditions. I'd take my hundred dollars for that week and invest in head shots. People got taken by these outfits all the time. We did a show about it on *Raymond,* when Robert's discovered as a model because he has a unique look, and he invests in head shots from the agency that signs him. He goes back to pick them up at the place, and it's now an empty room. That happened to some friends of mine.

Difficult time. Then I got an exciting job. My roommate, Rob Weiner, worked at the Metropolitan Museum of Art at the information desk and I became a guard there.

For about a year I was a security guard and over the course of that time I worked every shift. I worked the regular shift when the public was there, and I worked the four P.M. to midnight shift for a while, and then I worked the graveyard shift, midnight till eight in the morning.

It was amazing. I could go in after hours and turn on the lights in any gallery in one of the greatest museums in the world. You know the things written next to every painting? Those explanations you never have time to read because there are lots of people around? I had time to read every one.

I learned so much about art at that job and I learned a lot about the world. For example, did you know that any time there's a crime where art is stolen, the guards did it? This I know because I worked with these guys.

There were not too many actors working night security jobs at the Met. My fellow guards were just barely this side of the law, if not on the other side. Some of them were dangerous and scary and some of them were psychotic. And they all had lockers in the basement next to mine.

A couple of quick stories:

This one didn't happen on my watch, but it was legend at the museum. One guard broke into a case in the Egyptian Wing and took out Nefertiti's jewels and brought them over to a pawnshop on Eighty-sixth Street. And the pawnshop owner took one look at Nefertiti's jewels and said, "Where did you get these?"

The guy says, "My sister."

And Mr. Pawnshop calls the Metropolitan Museum of Art. He says, "You might want to come down."

The Met keeps this quiet because they don't want you to know that this is going on. You're not supposed to think that Humanity's Most Valuable Treasures are being protected by Man's Most Degenerate Specimens. This next story did happen to the guy whose locker was right next to mine. He was an artist, a painter. And he was crazy. After hours, he went up to Rembrandt's self-portrait, a priceless painting. He took out his keys and made a big diagonal slash across it. Then he called the security dispatch downstairs in the basement and said, "I just defaced a painting. What should I do?"

And they said, "Um, stay right there, please."

The restoration department is so brilliant, so expert, that this could be kept quiet. They restored it perfectly, and nobody ever knew about it. This is world news, isn't it? Why aren't you calling someone? Why did he do it? An artist, Rembrandt's self-portrait . . . you didn't have to major in psychology.

The worst of these stories was from the Costume Exhibit.

It had a show featuring costumes from Hollywood. To give you an idea of the kind of men we're talking about who worked after hours there . . . some of the guys became disgruntled and went downstairs and formed a circle around Greta Garbo's dress from *Camille* . . . and did the unspeakable onto it.

If you said "eww," "eww" is correct. So these were my buddies. My workmates.

The funny part is that the guards are actually redundant at the museum. The human guards are there to make the people who are paying their dues and coming to the parties feel better. All you need to protect the art is two guys sitting in dispatch downstairs with the cameras and laser beams and alarms.

It was a bizarre time, because meanwhile I was getting cast in little, nonpaying or paying-next-to-nothing Off-Off-Broadway things. So I had to move from the day shift to the evening shift, and as performances for the plays started, I finally went to the graveyard shift, which was aptly named because it was the spookiest. I thought that I could do it all because I was twenty-one, and I could survive this kind of life where I would rehearse all day, do a show in the evening, and then go to work.

I'll explain how it works at the graveyard shift because I have a story tied to this.

Let's say you and I are on route five in the American Wing for the night. We would have walkie-talkies, and for the first hour I would go on a specified route—just walking through the galleries and saying, "Route five at 7259," which corresponds to a phone on the wall. And extension 7259 would ring from downstairs and I'd say, "Check." Then dispatch would say, "Check." And on to the next gallery and phone.

They make sure you're actually where you say you are. They also need to know you're entering the Etruscan Urn Room or whatever, so they can shut the alarms down as you pass through. I would do that for an hour, and then I would sit at my post for the next hour while you went and did the same exact route. And that's how it works all night, you and I alternating. There are guards at every wing of the museum doing this.

So I'm in a play now, Shakespeare at the Meat and Potatoes Theater, which is the fourth floor of a decrepit warehouse on Thirty-eighth Street, perfect place for the parents to see their investment really pay off. We go from rehearsals into dress rehearsals and performances. I have just enough time to get from there to work the graveyard shift. There is no time in the day to sleep. I'm overbooked. I'm on my third day without sleep and I'm on cold medication. So I'm out of my mind, a zombie. Okay, about four in the morning I'm on the third floor of the American Wing and I finish my route with a half hour to spare. I could take a break. I hang up the last phone from dispatch, "Route five at 6397," and I turn and find myself in the Hart Room, a period room from the 1600s in the American Wing . . . and there's a bed. It's a three-hundred-year-old bed. And the last thing I remember is walking over to this bed. Honestly, I don't remember anything else. An hour and a half later the entire museum is looking for the guard who didn't return to his post. What happened to this guard? Is there a robbery? Did he steal something? Is he dead? All the supervisors are looking for the guard who didn't return to his post.

An hour and a half later, they find me. The big scary lady supervisor finds me sleeping, sprawled out—keys here, walkie-talkie there, flashlight here, a little drool on the pillow. I remember her shaking me awake and saying, "What are you doing?!" And I just remember groggily looking up at her and thinking, *How did she get in my room?* Then I realize where I am, and I am mortified. "Oh my God. Oh my God, I'm so sorry." She goes, "Get back to your post!" I leap up and say, "Oh my God, I'm sorry." This period room from the 1600s is very low. I turn and the door jamb is not where the door jambs are in the 1900s, and I smack my head and almost pass out leaving this room in a hurry. The next day, I get an infraction-of-rules report. It's like a ticket. "5:30 A.M. Did not return to post. Found sleeping on bed in Hart Room." And the Metropolitan Museum of Art is buzzing about this, especially the information desk. My roommate says, "I'm both proud and ashamed of you at the same time." There is only one room in the entire museum closed for the day, and that is the Hart Room, because they have to make sure that I didn't damage anything. So I get this rules infraction report and I think the incident is over.

I come to work the next night and I am greeted with "Mr. Balego wants to see you in his office." Mr. Balego was the head of the night watch. I go to his office, and he says to me, "Yeah, the curators are pretty upset." And I say, "I'm really sorry." And he says, "Yeah, well, listen. To you it's a bed, to me it's a bed . . . to them it's a work of art. You're fired."

I say, "Oh no. Oh, but . . . I love the museum."

I did love the museum. I couldn't believe that I was fired. It was so humiliating, first of all—I'm a bachelor of fine arts and I've sullied fine art. And to be fired! I didn't want to be fired. I loved it there. "I work at the Met," I'd say to women, leaving out the security guard part. At that moment, two of my scary buddies come to escort me, making sure that I clean out my locker and don't sleep on anything else. They escort me, at one A.M., out the back door of the museum and into Central Park. That's where they leave you. Not even on the Fifth Avenue side. Out the back. Again I was mortified. The next morning I call one of the curators of the American Wing and I say, "Hi, my name is Phil . . . and I'm the guard who fell asleep on the bed." And the lady goes, "Oh. Well, I hope next time you'll refrain from touching the art." And I say, "Well, there won't be a next time. I was fired." She says, "Oh. Well . . . good-bye now." She wasn't going to help me as much as I'd hoped.

I write a letter to the head of all security for the Met. His name was Mr. Gore, no relation, and it was a more intimidating name then. The union dictates that if you want a hearing you can have one. So I get to have a hearing to see if I could be reinstated.

I meet with my union representative, who works in the maintenance and repair shop downstairs. I go into his shop, and a large, bored man greets me. He asks, "What did you do?" And I tell him that I fell asleep on the bed during my shift.

A moment passes, and my union representative says, "What are you, a moron?"

I answer, "Yes, sir."

And he says, "All right. Lissen, we're going to get up dere, I do dis all de time. When we get up dere, I'm going to plead your case. I'm going to tell de guy all de mitigating factors and you're going to shut up. You're not going to say a word, all right? And den when I am all done and only when I am all done I will den turn to you and I will say, 'Now, do you have anyting to add?' And den, den, and only den, do you speak. All right? Do you got it?"

And I say, "Yeah."

And he goes, "You sure? Don't fuck me up dere."

I say, "Don't worry."

We go upstairs. Mr. Gore is sitting behind his desk. He's rather formidable. He's wearing a gun. He has my little letter, written on a nice note card from the museum gift shop, explaining my circumstances and apologizing.

And he says, "All right, go ahead."

My union representative begins for me, "Well, basically, he's guilty. He admits dat he did it."

And then he turns to me and says, "And now, if you have anyting to add."

I'm staring at him. That's it? What happened to alldemitigating factors?

That was it. And I just sat there, waiting for the appropriate amount of time to pass to let that laugh really sink in for God, my audience. And I say to my rep, "Thank you."

I turn to the Head of All Security and say, "Well, sir, I was, as my note explains, I was—"

He cuts me off. "I got your note. I got your note. Let me just tell you this. If this was the army and we were at war, you would be shot for what you did."

Now, I'd been out of work already for a week. It took a week to get this hearing. Why did I even come back? Just so they could scare me some more before kicking me out the back door again?

Mr. Gore continues, "And if this was peacetime you would at least be thrown in jail."

And he waits for my response.

I say, "Glad this isn't the army." What are you supposed to say? And I'm just thinking, *You know, it's over, why bother?* Everybody has his piece of the world that he's in charge of and he's going to run it like he's important. I pass that on to you should you find yourself in a similar situation.

And then Mr. Gore says, "So you were on cold medication?"

And I say, "Yes, sir, I have it with me."

"Let me see it."

I give it to him, an antihistamine.

He says, "I can see how this would make you drowsy. Am I going to have any more trouble with you?"

"What?"

He says, "You're not going to do anything like that again, are you?"

I say, "I guess not, what other museum would hire me?"

He says, "I'm going to reinstate you."

And I got my job back. It was great! Here's what wasn't great: The people on the night watch felt like their power had been usurped. I went over their heads, you see. No one ever appealed before. The big mean scary lady supervisor and her friends, some of the other guards, saw me as getting special treatment.

They made life very difficult for me.

They gave me the known bad routes and would then tell me to do the routes over. "Go around again." "Why?" "Just do what we say."

After a few weeks of this, one guy snapped at me, "Just do what I say, asshole."

And I finally said, "Hey, get off my back."

"What did you say, motherfucker?" And he slams the phone down and comes upstairs. Do you know the Met? Do you know the grand staircase when you first walk in? It leads to these giant European paintings, right there in this large hall. There's a huge mosaic marble table in the middle of the hall. This young man comes up the grand staircase and then proceeds to chase me around that table. He wants to beat me up. It's another comic scene that isn't quite as funny when it's happening.

As he chases me around, I'm asking him, "What did I do? I don't know what I did." I'm fumbling to call dispatch on my walkie-talkie as I'm running around the table. "This is an emergency. Could you send someone up here?"

Meanwhile, the very angry murderer decides to come *over* the table.

Just then, a seventy-eight-year-old man walks in . . . very slowly . . . as this maniac's got me backed up against *The Toilet of Venus* (Boucher, 1751). And my savior says to me, "All right, all right. Come on." Like I'm a big fairy for calling him, while Officer Kill the Jew is still on the loose. So obviously, that's it for me. The lesson is, after you fall asleep on a museum's three-hundred-year-old bed, they don't really want you anymore.

That was the first year on my own. But I got another job rather quickly at P. J. Bernstein's, which was a deli at Seventieth and Third. I knew Warren Anker, who was leaving his job managing the deli.

So here I am, twenty-one years old, and suddenly I'm managing a deli in Manhattan, a pretty good deli. You ever have coleslaw on a hot dog? Very nice.

I'd never worked at a deli before, but for some reason I could handle this. It was taking phone orders, dispatching the delivery guys, and running the cash register, the wait staff, and the counter men; from three to eleven P.M. It wasn't a giant place, but it was on the Upper East Side, the land of very demanding clientele. I grew to love that job, too. I also grew another fifteen pounds working there because I could eat whatever I wanted.

Until three P.M. every day, I was free. I usually went to the movies. I was the nerd who would line up two hours before the first show the day a Woody Allen movie opened. I'd wait in a snowstorm outside the Beekman Theater thinking, *I'm just glad to be alive at the same time Woody Allen is making movies.* He was making movies, and I was waiting on line. I wasn't getting auditions, I didn't have an agent. If you don't have an agent, you're not really going to get an audition. And until you're in something, good luck getting an agent, and even then, it's very rare they want to go out and see something. I didn't have the stomach for this life. I wanted someone who saw me in the school play to say, "Exactly what we want. Who knew coming to see *Twelfth Night* at Hofstra would find us such a Phil Rosenthal?"

I was such a Phil Rosenthal.

But I always stayed ambitious enough to want to better my life. An opportunity came up at the deli. This older lady, society lady, thin, a lot of makeup, a lot, fancied herself a real grande dame, but looked more like Milton Berle doing the "Geisha Girl" sketch. She would come to this Jewish deli and one day she asked me to take care of her dogs while she went away. So I said, "Fine." And she said, "If you come to my apartment, I'll show you how to do the dogs." It was a few blocks north of the deli. "And I'll set you up, and then you can either come by every other day, or you can stay there." Great. So I came to her apartment. . . . It's got those big ceramic leopards, chintz . . .

She showed me the dogs. They were in a bathroom off her bedroom, little Pomeranians—you know the kind, the yip-yip dogs. They were running around with newspaper on the floor and with little hair ribbons. I wouldn't have to walk them; they'd do what they did on the paper right there—I don't know, people are strange.

So this woman said to me, "Now, what I thought we would do is we'd order Chinese food and we'd sit in bed and the dogs would get to know you." And she gestured to her bed.

Excuse me?

All the blood left my face, and I began to perspire. I started backing up and said, "Y-you know . . . I have to tell you something. I'm not going to be able to do this."

And she said, "What?"

I said, "I wanted to tell you that my brother is coming into town this week and I'm not going to be able to do this. I need to be with my brother. He's sick. So I'm really sorry."

She knew that this was a bullshit excuse and got really offended and started screaming, "You get out of here! Just get out!" (I'm like the *Midnight Cowboy,* no?) I backed out of the apartment, tripping over a ceramic tribesman, and she never came in the deli again. Made me sad. I felt sad for her.

But listen, hey, at least a lady was interested in me.

That same week, I come to work at P.J.'s and the door is locked. Is it a holiday? Did I forget? What happened? The chairs are up, the lights are off. It was three in the afternoon. The guy from the fish store next door comes out. "You looking for Bill?"

And I said, "Yeah."

And he laughed. "He run away."

"What?"

He said, "He owe everybody money—milkman, fish man, meat man, bread man. You don't see him again. Ha-ha!"

Now, I needed that job, a hundred and eighty dollars a week plus all you could eat. All of a sudden I didn't have a job. Again.

I did get some extra work in soap operas once through a family connection and, I have to say, I was terrible. You know, the job is to sit in the background and literally be background. In fact, the job is called background. I wish you could see a tape of my appearance, because you'd see me mugging and wildly eating breadsticks in a restaurant behind good-looking people who are doing their lines on *The Edge of Night.* But this was my chance. You've got to be seen. Actors like me, when they come on my show now, I'll say, "Oh no, Bad Actor Theater in the back there. Oh no."

I know what they're doing because I did that.

I wanted to get seen. I was so desperate. But instead, I got a job bartending at Richoux of London in the basement of the Citicorp building. They asked if I could start in a couple of weeks, and I said sure.

Now, I didn't know how to bartend, but I figured two weeks would give me enough time to learn the *Mr. Boston* bartender's book. And I'm not an idiot, so I could see, here are the ingredients and here's how you make whatever anybody wants. So great. I'll practice my—but then I get a call that night, "You've got to come in tomorrow."

"What?"

"You've got to come in at lunch tomorrow. We have an emergency. The guy's out."

I'd like more time, but I've got my *Mr. Boston.*

I walk into lunch at Richoux of London. It is a big restaurant, and it's three-people thick at the bar. Waiters and waitresses coming from both sides, and I'm the only bartender. First thing to do is change into the Richoux uniform, brown polyester pants, a brown polyester vest, a brown polyester tie, a tan shirt, and brown shoes. So you literally look and feel like a piece of crap.

And now I get behind a real bar, and it's pandemonium. People really seem to need their drinks. I see an attractive young lady at the bar and I figure, okay, she looks nice, she'll be first.

"What would you like?"

"I'd like a pink squirrel."

"Coming right up."

I go right to my *Mr. Boston.* I look under P. Nothing. I look under S. I look under R for rodent drinks. I didn't know what the hell . . . I couldn't find this thing. Now the waiters and waitresses start ordering.

"I want a Richoux blah-blah-blah."

"What?"

I look at the menu. There's a full page of their specialty drinks that you can only get at Richoux of London, and all of them involve the blender. I start to turn red and perspire. Everyone hates me. Because they should—I don't know what I'm doing. This is the actor's nightmare. Or, in my case, the out-of-work actor's nightmare. You're suddenly a brownly dressed bartender and you don't know what drinks are, and everyone hates you. What could I do? I apologize and I come in after hours and learn everything. One day the boss, a tall, craggy, smoking lady sees me making a Bloody Mary, and pulls me aside, cigarette dangling from one of the cracks in her face, voice like a broken lawn mower.

"Listen, we don't put vodka in the Bloody Marys."

"Excuse me?"

"You take the bottle like this and you hold it up for the guy to see and then you bring the bottle under the bar, and put your finger over the spout while you pour. You hold your finger over the spout so nothing comes out. We make the mix extra spicy so they don't know that there's no vodka in it."

Can you imagine the joy she felt when she came up with that? She does the same thing with kids and pacifiers. You show 'em their binky, then you slip something extra spicy in there instead.

I never did the "vodka-saver." I'd show her that I was doing it and then leave my finger off it. Because I care about people. Especially drunk people who tip.

But you had to be careful with her; she could kill you. She was like Wallace Beery in a wig.

She fired me. I still miss the way she'd almost sing, "Dump the old olives in that bin and take 'em back to the cook."

So now I'm looking for another bartending job, and the temp agency sends me to a place called Singles on the Upper East Side.

Singles. Hey, maybe I'll meet somebody.

I get there, and there's a bunch of guys at the bar, and I'm cleaning the glasses and I'm getting people drinks. And I say to this one guy at the bar, "When do the girls get here?"

"Girls?" And then he laughs.

In the movie, another guy laughs, then another, then another, and then I'm Jodie Foster in *The Accused.*

That was a particularly low point for me.

I was very popular that evening. I was just so embarrassed. You can't go through the theater world and not meet a wide variety of people, but these were older guys in their fifties and sixties. And I was twenty-two behind the bar. But again, nice to be wanted.

1982. Why was life turning out like this? I'd get home, make myself one of those new quesadillas that were taking over the city, and there'd be a call from my parents. "Just want to know how it's going. We haven't heard from you in a few days. Any news?"

"Yeah, Ma, Arthur Miller and Leonard Bernstein are writing a show for me. We open Thursday."

"That's not true. Is that true? Max! We have to go into the city Thursday!"

They were very supportive.

The next morning I have an interview at a small movie company called Almi Pictures in midtown. Now, because I had been such a stud at school, I had been in charge of Program Board Films at Hofstra. I bought movies for the school to show on the weekends from companies like this one, so that I could watch movies all weekend. But I knew how it worked; if I could buy movies for the school, I could sell movies to the schools. And I'm close enough in age to the kid who's buying the movies that I'd be good at selling them.

I go into this place because I have a contact—someone I used to buy from—and he introduces me to the boss. I start in with my logic about how I know how the business works from the other side, and it's going well, but I'm not sure I'm getting the job, and then finally I explode, "Don't send me back to the gay bar, please!"

"Uh, listen, I am interviewing someone else this afternoon."

I stand up. "I am so much better than this guy you're seeing. You will never have a better salesman than me. I promise you. I'll work for less. You will not find anyone better than me at this job."

I don't know why—fear?—but he hired me.

It's a small movie distribution company, and I start off by selling to colleges and I'm somewhat successful at it. Acting is on the back burner, although I'm still pursuing it, but I have a nine-to-five job. I work hard. In Times Square. I'm making almost $300 a week. I go to Nathan's with a coupon. "Three hot dogs for the price of two" (very smart to eat three hot dogs for lunch), or I get a nice lunch around the corner at the Greek deli. I have to tell you this: You wait on line there, cafeteria-style with your tray, and there are little signs that tell you what things are. "Half chicken, $3.25." One day I say to the guy, "I'll have the chicken."

The fellow says in his thick accent, "You want potato?"

I hesitate because I'm on a budget.

"Is okay," says my friend. "It go wit' it."

"Oh, great," I say. "Sure, potato, thank you."

I get to the front of the line. The cashier rings me up.

"Chicken . . . potato . . . $4.75."

"I'm sorry," I say. "He said the potato goes with it."

And the cashier says, "Yes. It go wit' it. It don't come wit' it."

Brilliant. These fellows have worked an accent scam.

The next day, I go back, to make sure.

"I'll have the chicken."

"You want potato?"

"Does it come with it?"

He's stuck. A moment. Then, shyly, "No . . . but it go wit' it."

As if to say, "It's a lovely aesthetic complement to your entrée."

I have found that New York is indeed a Benneton ad, filled with adorable crooks of every ethnic variety.

Soon the folks at Almi Pictures recognized my passion for the movies. It was a small enough place; they'd acquired a couple of libraries that included movies like *Swept Away, Seven Beauties,* and other foreign films, and horror movies. They distributed movies that were either very highbrow or very lowbrow, but what all their films had in common was that they weren't popular enough for anyone else to want.

They sold them in art houses and schlock houses around the country. I was so passionate about what I was doing and so interested that soon I was doing acquisitions work. I would go to see screenings of films that didn't have distributors and since I was the target audience—I was the youngest guy in the company at twenty-three—after being there a year, I was head of acquisitions and marketing. To save money, they let me write and edit trailers. There was a funny horror one for an awful movie called *Superstition*—it had to be funny because that was the only possible way to sell it—and I cast Brother Theodore (a frequent guest on the NBC *Letterman* show) to do the voice-over. He was hilarious. And this thing became a cult trailer—it showed midnights at the Eighth Street Playhouse before *The Rocky Horror Picture Show.* I went downtown to see it one night, and people were calling out to the screen in response to Theodore. I guess that was my first professional writing job. It was a kick to have a whole audience laughing at something I wrote and put together, even if it was for this terrible, terrible movie that no one under any age should be allowed to see.

Still, I couldn't give up acting completely. My roommate was a directing major at Columbia University's graduate school, and they didn't have an acting program. So after work I was an actor for the directing classes and shows. The writing classes needed actors, and I would get to be in these great directing and writing classes with these fantastic professors and guest directors like Alan Schneider, and that's how I went to Columbia's graduate school for two years, for free. I recommend this.

And then something happened. Some underclass friends of mine from Hofstra were doing a play downtown and invited me. Onstage with them was an actress I never saw before. She was hilarious. She was like a cross between Judy Holliday and Carol Burnett and Imogene Coca, but in a very nice package. I sent word backstage with my friends because I was a little intimidated to talk to her myself. I said, "Tell that girl she's funny." And I left.

Two weeks later, I'm walking down the street during one of New York's great annual events, the Ninth Avenue Food Festival—they close off the street from Thirty-seventh to Fifty-seventh streets, and it's wall-to-wall food of every ethnicity. This I also recommend. And I'm walking with a buddy, carrying a giant, dripping beef rib in my hand like a malnourished caveman, and who comes walking toward me from the other direction, but the actress. The cute, funny girl. And she's with a friend of hers I know from school. We stop and say hello, and we're formally introduced. It turns out she transferred to Hofstra after I had graduated, and that's why we hadn't met before. And I say, dripping sauce on my Joe Jackson *Jumpin' Jive* T-shirt, "I'm a big fan of yours." And she smiles and says right back to me, "I'm a big fan of yours, too."

Wow. She knew my work. I was quite a legend at Hofstra with my Shakespearean Andrew Aguecheek and my commedia dell'arte turn as Pancrazio in back-to-back performances in one semester. . . .

Turns out she was lying. She never saw me or my work. But she liked me, or was desperate, or something was wrong with her in the head. And that was it. A couple of days later, my roommate is having trouble casting a part in this show we're doing up at Columbia. Tom McGowan and I are in it, and we need a funny girl. I think of this Monica Horan I just met. I call her, she reads for the part, gets it, we rehearse, get to know each other, and she takes advantage of me.

Monica was like a wonderful good luck charm. Two weeks after meeting her, the company I worked for, Almi Pictures, went out of business, and I was out of work again.

I had lasted at Almi for three years before Monica's curse. Al and Mi decided they wanted to be in another business, and they closed up shop and sold off the library. Now, Miramax was just starting up at the same time. I interviewed with Harvey Weinstein and his brother and, with all due respect, they were insane maniacs.

It was kind of a schlocky office, and they were doing the same thing that our company was doing—just grabbing whatever movie they could and trying to sell it. It's an ugly business, but you could win an Oscar. One of Almi's movies won an Oscar for best foreign film, *The Official Story.* I had worked on the ad campaign for it, which got me in the door at Miramax. At one point in the interview, which I thought was going well, Harvey Weinstein said, "So you want this job?"

"Yes, sir, I'm very interested in movies."

"What do you want to do after this?"

"Nothing. I'm interested in movies. I love the movies."

"LIAR! YOU'RE A LIAR!" He was suddenly, inexplicably, screaming at me.

Then the brother jumps in. "You work at this other place and you're here and you're spying for them!"

"No, sir. That place closed. I want a job here."

But truthfully, because of the crazy yelling, no, I don't want a job here. I ran out.

They just frightened me. They still frighten me.

So I had no job, and Monica, very wisely, decided that I was the right person to move in with. I don't know what she was thinking. Maybe she wanted to finish me off, but I knew she was right for me. It wasn't BOOM—THE THUNDERBOLT! It was, "Ah, yes, this is right. After all this time, finally, this is whom I'm supposed to be with. A perfect fit. No alterations. Never going to have to take it back. I will probably marry this girl. I just have to be able to take care of her. But before I do that, I should be able to at least cover my half of the $300 rent in Washington Heights."

Some other friends of mine from college had been asking me to join their theater improv group. I was pretty good at improvisation. But the problem I always had with improvisation is that it can't be great every time. You take a chance. And to me, that's like taking a chance with a gun. If you want to kill yourself, fine, but you don't do it in front of an audience. One year I saw something my friends did that was pretty good. I said, "You know what? Could I be in the next thing?" Nothing was going on for me anyway and they're nice, funny people, so why not? So we actually wrote this thing through improvised rehearsals, and it became a big hit for our little group. We got on the cover of the weekend section of the *New York Times.* Then we moved to a bigger theater, a bit swankier, celebrities were coming—and I was getting paid for this.

So now what would the next show be? Well, my friends had experimented with a piece that they did a couple of times that needed a lot of work. They had tried this improvisational show on certain weekends, but it had no shape to it, no structure at all. Now they wanted to revisit it because we were a success with this other project.

I was to play a pretty good role in this show but I was not taking chances. No improvisation for me—people were paying. I wrote a big chunk of the play, and it actually became successful. (I don't want to plug the name of this show because I don't see a dime from it, and if it's okay with you, I'd like to spend the rest of the book complaining about that.)

When it started out, it was just going to be a few weekends. And the woman who started the group—let's call her Tootie—the moment she saw her own photo in the *New York Times* she became a monster. She took full credit for the play and, as Mel Brooks's Two-Thousand-Year-Old-Man said about Robin Hood, stole from everybody, kept everything. She resented anybody else who was getting a laugh in her show. It became a scary time. Tootie thought that the piece's success came about because she had *chanted* for success. Oy.

When we opened, I got very nice reviews, and it was a good showcase for me. It was the biggest hit I'd been involved with, and at twenty-seven, I was a working actor. Honestly, it's not great or even good theater, this show. But we were the toast of the town and things were going very well—a dream realized. We were running for almost a year, eight shows a week, and Tootie was getting ready to take this show to Hollywood and be a star. We started hearing that she was maybe taking too much credit for writing our play. And slowly, we noticed people were starting to get fired. The last straw for me came when Tootie went on *Live at Five* on WNBC and Chuck Scarborough said, "Let's take a look at a clip." The clip they showed was me. Tootie was livid.

One weekend, I had Tom McGowan's wedding to attend in Texas, and before I went I was to instruct my understudy how to do my part. He tape-recorded my performance to learn it. Because it all had started so informally, I was the only one who kept my part on paper, because I had written it. He got my part down, and when I returned, I was fired. Right before the show went to Hollywood. The only explanation I got was, "You're like a country-western cut on our jazz album."

I was devastated. I couldn't believe it. It had been so hard to even get an audition for a show, let alone cowrite one, be in it, and then have it go on to such a triumph. It was what I wanted to do my whole life and it was suddenly, stunningly, cruelly, over.

Not only that, no one in the show called me or stood up for me, because they were afraid they'd be next. I lost my friends. Absolutely, up until then, this was the worst thing that had ever happened to me. Other friends and family at the time said, "Well, you learned something about people." Can I tell you something? This was a lesson I would have rather gone through life not learning, but maybe it was an early glimpse of "Hollywood." I guess you should never work with your friends.

The show is still running, but the group has disbanded. Many people sued Tootie and are still suing her. The trimmed-down-for-profit version of the show did come to Hollywood. The core group did get to make a pilot of it for a television show. It failed. They somehow got another chance with it. It failed again. They blamed one another. She blamed everybody. It was just a mess of lawsuits and bad feelings. The smartest thing I ever did, and what became the turning point in my life, was that I put that behind me and never looked back.

Until today. For the book. Where I'm supposed to look back.

3

Paramus with Palm Trees

I hope you didn't just buy that crap about "putting it all behind me," because I didn't. I didn't sue Tootie, but only because I had no money to sue. What I did was the poor man's version of suing—I got incredibly depressed.

It was debilitating, actually. I didn't know what the hell to do with myself.

Then I remembered that somebody who had seen me in the show, an agent from Hollywood, had said, "If you come to Los Angeles you will never stop working as an actor." So, like a schmuck, I moved to Los Angeles, and I never started working as an actor. I had said to Monica, "I've got to go try this for a couple months." She gave me her blessing. I had $300. I packed a suitcase, flew to Los Angeles, walked into the agent's office, and Jimmy "J.J." Walker, who was then ten years past being one of the hottest stars in sitcoms, was standing there. My guy represents him. A good sign, I think.

The agent says, "Can't believe you're here. It's so great. We're going to get you working. Now listen, here's what we're going to do: My associate is going to handle you."

I say, "Oh, but, I don't know her."

"Yes, yes, but I want her to be as excited about you as I am."

I say, "How's that going to work? She hasn't seen me in anything."

"Don't worry about it. I'll show her a tape of you, and it's going to be great. You will never stop working as an actor."

I went from very depressed in New York to rock-bottom depressed in Los Angeles.

I was a Woody Allen New Yorker. He taught me what to think about LA before I ever got here, and when I got here, I thought he had been kind. The old saying was true: There's no "there" here. It's suburbia without the urbia. It may be paradise, but you can't see it for all the smog and strip malls.

I stayed in an apartment on Beachwood Drive, under the Hollywood sign, on a couch belonging to my friend Alan Kirschenbaum. Alan was already a comedy writer, was working on *Dear John* for Ed. Weinberger (producer of *The Mary Tyler Moore Show, Taxi, The Cosby Show*). Alan was a friend of mine from high school. His father is Freddy Roman, the great Catskills comedian. Freddy used to take us up to the Catskills with him on gigs. We got to go backstage, and he'd say to us, "Hey, you see the soap opera section of the paper? Circle some of the soap operas that sound funny, the little digests of what happens, we'll talk about them, and we'll see if we can work them into the act." We were excited. We thought we were writing his act at fifteen, sixteen years old. We got such a thrill because here was this comedian going up onstage doing what we had been going over with him moments before. So that stayed with me. Alan Kirschenbaum was a dear friend. And he was very funny. And he had a couch.

By the way, Freddy Roman's joke is, "When I entered show business, and my family saw the act, they changed their name to Kirschenbaum."

Alan had been a year behind me in high school, and we had

been in plays and comedy groups together. He had had some success breaking into writing while we were still in New York. He wrote a spec script that was great for Garry Shandling's show. He got an agent and he got a job on the staff of another TV show. But the job was very disheartening to him. He hated it and he said to me, "We're funnier than the people on this show. We should write something."

Alan came to my apartment one day with this heavy blue metal box. "It's called a word processor," he said.

He had an idea for a screenplay about a suburban detective. We decided he'd be from our hometown of New City. We knew that world. We named the detective Shulman after the man who lived up the street from me growing up, because we loved the sound of his name: Millard Shulman. We envisioned this role for Alan Arkin, our favorite actor. An aside: There's a movie called *Big Trouble* that is not very wonderful except for Alan Arkin's spit take in it. (For the novice, a spit take is an action taken by the actor in which he or she ingests a certain amount of food or drink, only to be surprised before swallowing what's in the mouth, causing the food or drink to be ejected out of the mouth, causing joy among all who are not in range.) Everyone who sees Alan Arkin in this movie agrees, this is the world's greatest spit take. He does it just after Peter Falk has given him some "sardine liquor." I won't ruin it for you, but rent that movie. So while I was in that unhappy play in New York, we wrote *Shulman.* There was a part in it for me, and we loved working on it. We showed it to people, and they seemed to like it. Alan's agent, a young man named Adam Berkowitz, had to represent me at the William Morris Agency for this screenplay because Alan and I wrote it together.

He sent *Shulman* around, and HBO liked it—they'd see if it could be cast. "What do you mean, 'Could be cast'? We wrote it for Alan Arkin." And they told us: "No, no. Alan Arkin doesn't open a movie."

My first Hollywood lesson: You may love him; he may be perfect; he may be the funniest actor on the planet. Nobody cares. He's not "bankable." Is there a word more stifling to the creative process? "Bankable."

This was not easy for me to accept, because, having just been fired from the unhappy show, I was not so bankable, either. But since I was desperate, I just wanted the thing cast.

All I did was harass Alan. "Did you hear anything about the movie?" I needed this. I was in New York with nothing, and then I was in LA with less than nothing. I was renting a very used car from Ugly Duckling and living on a couch. The couch was faster.

All I can say is, thank God for my friends, because I would probably be typing this on a used word processor without them. One day I was walking to a meeting in Century City when I was first out here, 1989. I was walking, and I was actually commenting to myself, "Nobody walks here." It was so weird to me. And as I was walking, a lady walked past me and I heard "Phil Rosenthal?" I turned and said, "Patti Chafitz? Who I haven't seen in fifteen years since high school?"

She said, "What are you doing out here?" I said, "I'm trying to be an actor." She said, "What, are you still acting?" "Yeah, and I wrote this thing." "Oh," Patti said, "finally someone I know whom I can help." I said, "What do you do?" She said, "I'm an entertainment lawyer in this building." And she pointed to the building they filmed *Die Hard* in.

Patti played bass fiddle in the orchestra of the shows we did in high school. Wonderful girl, a year ahead of me, brilliant and, it turned out, a very successful entertainment lawyer. So we're talking on the street there, and I said, "By the way, if you know anybody who needs a housesitter, I'm available." I'm going from couch to couch and I have nowhere to live. She said, "Do you like dogs?" and I said, "No, no, no, I'm not asking if I can live with you." She said, "Come and see my house."

I went to see her house. She had a big house with her husband in Silver Lake. There was a bedroom with its own bathroom, and I could stay there. She didn't care; she did this for people. Patti (now Felker) and her husband (Mr. Felker) didn't have any kids yet. They had a big German shepherd named Dweeble. If I walked the dog, it was worth it to them for me to stay there. They were both very busy; they were hardly ever there; and they had a swimming pool. Nice. The last person who stayed in that room was her friend Dean. I met Dean, and the following week Dean won an Oscar for Best Live Action Short Film, which he did with Steven Wright. I'm thinking, *This is a good room.* Dean Parisot went on to direct *Galaxy Quest* and many other fine features. I went on to live in that room. And I walked the dog. I'll say this about Los Angeles, it's easier to be unemployed here than in New York. I'm depressed, have no money, and thinking about what a failure I am, while floating every afternoon in a swimming pool.

I went to some meetings. Patti couldn't even really help me professionally in any way. What could she do? How can you be an entertainment lawyer for someone who's not in the entertainment business?

And then a guy whose plays I had been in at Columbia's grad school, Oliver Goldstick, called me and said, "I hear you're out here, I've been trying to break into the sitcom business, would you want to write a spec with me?" ("Spec" means on your own, for no money—on speculation.) I had never written a sitcom script before, so I asked Alan to tell me the basic structure of one over lunch at a perfectly terrible seafood restaurant on Melrose Avenue. And here it is as it's been handed down for generations, to Ed. Weinberger, to Alan Kirschenbaum, to me over lunch in about ten minutes, and now to you:

There are three crucial structural elements to the well-made sitcom script, and they are as strict as a haiku.

The most important element is the premise. What is the story about? Not a small question. Is it worth doing a whole show about this?

The second most important element—and I couldn't guess this—the act break. The act break is the end of the first act, right before the commercial in the middle of the show. It's what the first act has led up to, and what all the action of the second act will stem from. It gives people a reason to keep watching. A classic act break line is, "We're getting married."

And the third most important element is . . . the conclusion. Was it worth driving all this way for this?

That's it. Of course, these sitcom elements are simply a beginning, a middle, and an end, and are the basis of all good storytelling. It's just that in a sitcom, you have twenty-two minutes between commercial interruptions—there's not a lot of room for anything else. The story must always be driving forward. The audience should not be aware of the structure while they're watching, they should just be entertained, but subconsciously, the strength of the story's structure will make the episode resonate with them far more than an unformed collection of jokes and funny faces. It's what made the classics we love, like *The Honeymooners,* what they are, and what I've tried to emulate in my own work.

Armed with this knowledge, Oliver and I decided to write a *Roseanne* script. The story we landed on is about John Goodman's character getting another job—he's moonlighting on the graveyard shift at the local museum when he falls asleep on a three-hundred-year-old bed.

There was a slight difference from my personal story—with him, the bed collapses. That was our act break.

People really seemed to respond to this wild, imaginative story. How did we think of this?

We sent it to Adam Berkowitz in New York, and he said if he could get an agent out there in Los Angeles to like it as well, then maybe we could do something. He sent it to a woman named Liz

Robinson in the Los Angeles office of William Morris, and she called, and they signed us. We were signed within a week of submitting that script. So within six months of moving out to LA, I had my first job as a television writer. Yes. Oliver and I were partners, and we shot right to the top on our very first show, the Robert Mitchum sitcom.

Alan had told me that what you learned from your first show, you could learn from any show. Meaning: Get the job—any job—and learn how the business works, the sitcom business specifically. *A Family for Joe*, starring Robert Mitchum, was certainly "any job." It was also very bad.

But I was very naive and so excited, and thinking that, yes, Robert Mitchum may not be perfect for a sitcom but he's Robert Mitchum. At the first meeting with the other, more senior, writers I said, "Isn't this fantastic? Robert Mitchum. *Night of the Hunter.*" And I got a blank look from these people . . . these people who are in show business. They'd never seen the movie.

So I said, "You're going to come over and see *Night of the Hunter* because you have to see it if you're going to work with Robert Freakin' Mitchum." Now, I was half a staff writer, which is the lowest level, but they all came over. I had the video of *Night of the Hunter* and I think it's safe to say it's one of the best movies ever made. It's the only movie that Charles Laughton ever directed. It's the only screenplay by James Agee. If you haven't seen it, you have to put the book down again and go rent this movie right now.

But . . . because it's stylized and somewhat dreamlike and nightmarish in a surrealistic way, my guests that night laughed at it. My heart was breaking. They laughed at it and as they left the house they were saying, "Great movie, Phil," and snickering. I actually remember thinking, *Oh, no. They're all dopes. What have I gotten into?* I was in the land of crap. *Night of the Hunter* is undisputed. This is a great work of art, this movie. Maybe working in television would not be the experience I had hoped for.

However . . . I had a job. I sent for Monica. Patti and Monica had already become fast phone friends over the few months I had been there. It was Patti's idea that I have Monica come out and stay with us awhile. I picked Monica up at LAX, and as we were driving over to Patti's, I was telling her all about the exciting world of television, and how we had started to write scripts, and all she was hearing was "bluh, bluh, bluh." This was not just because I'm very boring . . . she was fuming because "All he cares about is TV. What about how he promised that when he got a job we'd get married? This idiot is stringing me along." What she didn't realize was that at that moment, this idiot had a ring in his pocket and was driving her up to Griffith Park.

I made up some excuse, that we had to pick up someone, which also seemed to annoy her, and to kill time, why don't we look at the view from the observatory at sunset?

"Whatever, fine," she said. We got up there, and I took her to "the spot" and I had started to dig into my pocket when a horde of Japanese tourists came around the corner, taking pictures of the scenery. I said to Monica, "Um, let's look at the view from over here . . ." and we moved. Sure enough, more tourists. "Hey, let's go over here. . . ."

We moved about five times as I tried to find a secluded spot. Each time we moved, I could feel my audience slipping away. The mood was leaving. Finally, I found a place with only a few people around, and I got down on one knee. "What are you doing?" said Monica, panicking in embarrassment. I said, "I love you, Monica. Will you marry me?" And Monica, very sweetly, said, "Huh?"

I repeated the question. "Will you please marry me? People are starting to look." And the Japanese were starting to fire.

"Uh-huh," said my future wife. I put the ring on.

"Wrong finger," she said. Second attempt . . . I got it right, and we've lived happily ever after. I later learned that the spot I wound up proposing in was actually quite auspicious; it was the very location of the knife fight in *Rebel Without a Cause,* and, thirty years later, the exact same spot where Arnold Schwarzenegger, as *The Terminator,* ripped a young man's heart right out of his chest.

Given my track record with women, I was very lucky neither of those things happened to me there. Monica and I stopped at the supermarket and picked up some bridey type magazines for my future bride, and we went "home" to Patti's house.

A Family for Joe had started as a 1989 TV movie on NBC. It was about a homeless man, Robert Mitchum, who lives in a cardboard box in Central Park. You with me? When recently orphaned children happen upon him in the park, they ask him if he will pretend to be their grandpa so that they will not be split up and put into foster homes, in exchange for which he gets a roof over his head.

This television movie was the highest-testing *anything* in NBC history—more than *The Cosby Show,* more than *Cheers,* more than anything. And because of these test numbers, they couldn't just leave it alone. They had to do something more with it. The movie was not even really a comedy. It was what the networks actually called a warmedie—like one of those Hallmark Special things, but we were supposed to make it a sitcom in front of a live audience. So that was weird, too. But I'm thinking . . . the premise is not terrible. If Robert Mitchum plays it as Robert Mitchum, or like W. C. Fields, and he hates little kids and dogs, you might have a shot at something because he's a curmudgeon, and he can be funny in this situation. We can make Robert Mitchum funny, I think.

The first moment of the first episode, filmed in front of an audience, is an empty stage set of a suburban house and you hear *ding-dong.* And then a deep voice. "I'll get it." It's Robert Mitchum offstage. And then Robert Mitchum emerges from the kitchen wearing an apron and holding a vase with flowers, which he puts on the table and adjusts before he goes to answer the door.

The series was finished right there, dead. They took his balls off in the first moment of the show. Why? Because they didn't want him to be scary. They didn't want him to be threatening. They didn't want him to be unlikable. So, dead.

It didn't matter what else we did. I was sitting there, knowing nothing, never having worked in this medium, but I knew, you would know, Crazy Oma would know, that that was a mistake. The legendary Brandon Tartikoff, who was in charge of programming at NBC, took one look at this first episode and said, "It should be cut up and made into guitar picks." *A Family for Joe* lasted seven episodes.

During that time, though, Monica and I went and got married in her hometown in Pennsylvania, in the same hall where her parents got married, and I have to say, the food wasn't very good. We did a first dance, however, that was very popular with the guests—we choreographed a whole number that started out like a tango and then got all fast and crazy. I tell you these details not just because these are some of my favorite memories, but because almost every experience I'm writing about here will somehow be used later. You'll see. And what you'll also see is that as you go through life as a writer, it's easier to write things down than to actually write. Whatever I couldn't put in a show, I tried to learn from the experience—what to do . . . and quite a bit of what not to do.

Baby Talk, our second sitcom job, gave us a terrific lesson in that department. Alan Kirschenbaum, who had been working for Ed. Weinberger on *Dear John,* would be second in command for Ed. on *Baby Talk.* Alan convinced Ed. to hire Oliver and me, and I was thrilled to work for such a legend as Ed. Mr. Weinberger does not disappoint—he's hilarious, dry, quick, outrageously funny, with a famous voice that's somewhere between a whine and a grumble. But this project, this show, I couldn't figure out. It was going to be the TV version of the hit movie *Look Who's Talking,* and I didn't know nothin' 'bout birthin' no babies. We even told Ed. that this wasn't really our bailiwick, but he had another show that would be in development, a sitcom starring Ray Sharkey, from *Wiseguy,* who would play a tough guy forced to come back and take care of his family.

This is more up our alley. Ed. says, "Okay, so we'll help each other." And that meant we'd be on *Baby Talk* first.

Now, I believe the way they made the movie *Look Who's Talking* was like this: A group of comedy writers sat in a room, looking at hours and hours of baby footage, and when it looked like the baby had an expression on his face to which a specific idea could be attached, the writers would come up with the baby's inner dialogue to be recorded later by Bruce Willis.

The way we were told to do *Baby Talk* was like this: We would write scripts, and the babies would perform them live in front of a studio audience every week.

Surprisingly, the first week went poorly. The second week was like a train derailment. A train derailment where the train is filled with exploding manure, and no one in town escapes without throwing up. Ed. fired the babies the third week . . . for crying. When we told him that's what babies do, he told us that wasn't the only reason he was letting the babies go. They also wanted off on the Jewish high holy days, and he didn't believe the parents. "You're telling me those kids are going to be in temple, the way they carry on?" I loved Ed. George Clooney was the star of *Baby Talk* when it premiered in 1990, and I loved George, too. He's truly one of the great, even heroic, guys in show business and has only gotten nicer with success. (This has happened maybe one other time.) But I think it's fair to say, and George himself has said this, he wasn't crazy about the show. One day during a rehearsal, he and Ed. had a somewhat heated argument that resulted in George's cursing in front of everyone and throwing the script across the stage. "It's not you with your shlong hanging out up here, Ed.!" said George Clooney. Silence. Ed. took the writers upstairs to the office. "His shlong hanging out?" grumbled Ed. "That's where he goes for his metaphors?" He ran his hand through his wild mane of side-of-the-head hair. "I think next week his character gets married and moves to Africa."

The next week George Clooney's character got married and moved to Africa. We had a tribal ceremony with drums in the show, and *Baby Talk* said good-bye to George Clooney. I'll never forget Ed.'s prophetic words, "Let him do a pilot every year for the rest of his life, that'll be his career." There are so many great Ed. stories, they will have their own book someday.

The other one I have for you was on the next show—the Ray Sharkey one. (I don't have to tell you what happened to *Baby Talk,* do I?) But first, you'd like a career in television, wouldn't you? Let's go over a typical week on any one of these shows I worked on—and this experience is not just limited to these shows. This is how a week goes by on most TV shows:

Monday. The table read. This is the first time the script is read out loud by the cast, usually sitting around a table, while the writers and crew listen and, you hope, laugh. The table read isn't very good because the whole premise of the show isn't very good, and the script was written over the last couple of weekend nights because last week's script needed so much work, there wasn't a lot of time to devote to this week's script. You'll see how we come back around to this the following week, like Sisyphus. Truth is, the script was probably good enough for this facachta show, and as we're about to walk back to the office to put some Band-Aids on it, the network, or the studio, or even the executive producer might say, "Well, I think we need a story." A story? If somebody says story at this late point in the process, you know what that means. This is a page-one rewrite. Yes. You're going back to work on the story, maybe a new story. That's, "Oh, no." I can't tell you how many nights—long, pointless, frustrating, fattening nights—I had over five years of "Oh, no."

Page-one rewrite. The cast has gone home—no point in rehearsing a script that's been thrown out. Now it's Monday, and we're shooting this show Friday. But we have to think of a new story and write a whole new script by tomorrow. This means we're going to split up and each take a scene, then we're going to meet back in The Room (The Writers' Room) at about ten P.M. and rewrite and cobble together the whole thing so it kind of makes sense. At that moment you get a pit in your stomach like there's a math test tomorrow you didn't study for, plus your paper is due on *Moby-Dick,* which you didn't read, plus you're naked.

Most shows are like that.

And this might be one good reason why most television is terrible.

How good is that script going to be the next day?

What I've learned: Nothing was ever funny at three in the morning. You just thought it was. Because you were punchy and loopy from not sleeping, eating candy, and drinking soda.

Some rooms do other things.

Tuesday. So you come in the next day. If the writers have managed to come up with a new script, the actors have got to do a table reading again in the morning. They're either scared to death because they now have *four* days to learn a show, or they've become so used to this process they don't care anymore; the script doesn't have their full attention because, under the table, they've got their agents on the phone working on what's next.

Neither attitude makes for a good show.

This Tuesday table read is usually not *Masterpiece Theatre,* either—how could it be? The new script was written in one night. What do we do now? Why don't we go back to more rewriting? The actors are going to go through the motions of rehearsing, and we're going to come to a run-through at the end of the day, at four or five P.M. We're going to come and see it "on its feet" (the actors literally up on their feet, walking about the set with scripts in hand).

We see it on its feet, and this, too, is usually terrible. Now, the writer has an opportunity at this point to give notes to the director, who would then pass them on to the actors. But rather than giving notes to the director or the actors on how to fix the staging or the intentions so they might work, most writers don't know how to do that or don't want to do that. The writers' solution: rewrite. And so you have another "Oh, no," as in "Oh, no, we're going to be here till three in the morning again."

How are you physically and emotionally at this moment?

With any luck, you're young enough to live.

Everybody's tired, but the ideas must keep coming.

It's your job. You're getting paid more money than you ever thought you would make in your life. If you're getting $1,000 a week, you're saying, "Holy shit, $1,000 a week. Holy shit. I was making $300 a week before this. I'm now a thousandaire."

Our culture has led us to believe that to get any job in television or movies is magical. But please, get a sense of just how nuts it is and how hard you work. I mean, imagine . . . say to most people, "Sit in a room until you have a very good idea." I think they'd freak out. This is what the writer faces every single day.

And what's a good idea? I don't know what a good idea is. Whose criteria is it? My idea of a good idea or your idea of a good idea? Since I'm putting you in The Room and I'm going to pay you, you have to come up with my idea of a good idea. And that idea then has to mesh with everybody else's idea. Your idea could be, and most of the time is, rejected. A choice most writers then opt for is pouting.

Wednesday. Same thing again, maybe to a lesser degree, but there's still a ton of rewriting to do. And you do it, and it's very late. Very late at night. You come home and walk into bed with your clothes on and try to sleep for an hour or two before whoever's next to you—or, God forbid, a child—wakes you up.

Thursday. Thursday is camera blocking, and that's almost a reprieve, because you can't really change that much on camera-blocking day. Because they're setting it now for the cameras, it would be counterproductive to change it too much. You would think. On one particular series, however, the executive producer would get his old partner, bring him into his office privately and rewrite everything we had done all week. The day before the show. At least Thursday wasn't going to be a late night—unless we were behind on next week's script, which . . . how could we not be?

So Thursday is spent doing that, and you begin to slowly run out of caring.

Friday. Show day. We go to a final run-through in the morning, and that's usually a bus crash. You have to do some rewriting between that thing and the show. An audience comes in. *Really?* you think. *People are actually coming to see this?* If you're not a hit show, this audience is comprised of nursing home inhabitants and street gangs who are being rehabilitated by having a night out for what our society advertises as fun. The show should take about three hours to film, but if you're in trouble it can be five to six. Some shows regularly have a seven-hour taping. Why? The show doesn't work, and they're now writing between scenes. They're actually writing new scenes—between scenes while the studio audience waits, and starts thinking, *This is not as delightful as I thought it'd be. Let's kill that old lady.*

So Friday's a very late night. That's four out of five very late nights every week. And you never catch up. That's why you might have to come in on Saturday. And maybe Sunday. Because you don't have next week's script ready, which will bring you back to . . . Monday.

Does it have to be this way? Well, if the guy who runs the show's (the showrunner's) home life is such that he doesn't want to go home, that's another reason why you might stay late—even if you don't really have to—because the showrunner does not want to go home to that wife or those kids. Or that empty room with the soup and the stack of pornography.

He won't even start working until the evening. So you're at his mercy. And then there are the people who are running shows who have no business doing that because they are not ready to run a show yet. They were on staff of a hit show and sold a pilot. But they don't know what they're doing and don't know what they want and they're operating from fear and nervousness. Their minds are changing all the time because they just don't know what they want. Or they're listening to the network's or the studio's notes and assuming they know what they want. You have to know what *you* want.

The one other thing that'll keep you there long hours—and this is the most dangerous—is the Petulant Star. If you have the Petulant Star, there'll be a table reading, and everybody could think it's great. The Petulant Star takes the script and throws it on the floor and says, "I'm not doing this."

Now what? "Well, what would you like, sir or madam?"

"Think of something." Walks out. That's happened to me on several shows. Sometimes there's more than one Petulant Star, each demanding his or her own story line, or to wear a bathing suit onscreen. The writers get batted around. The only solace you can take is in knowing that as a writer, you may soon work again on something else. The actor probably will not.

Sometimes all of the above maladies congregate in one place, on one show. And it is from this perfect storm on the Ray Sharkey vehicle *The Man in the Family* that my last Ed. story for this volume comes.

Wednesday run-through. It's late, about nine P.M. The actors and the director never stay this late during the week, but this particular script was in particularly bad shape, so they didn't get the new pages until very late in the day Wednesday. They'd been working all day and night, and we'd all come down to see if this new stuff worked at all on its feet. The director is John Rich, a television giant who directed many classics, including *All in the Family.* John is a large, large, red-faced man with white hair, short patience, and a gruff but not unpleasant demeanor. I liked him.

He leaned on a podium as rehearsal commenced, and, since it was on wheels, leaned on it to kind of ride his formidable belly over to the next set for the following scene. It was going well tonight, which meant there was no actual odor coming from the work. As the actors finished their third scene, at about ten P.M., Ed. casually remarked to John, "What are they, tired?"

John stared at Ed. in disbelief. "Tired?" he said in a low, even tone. "Tired?" he repeated in a tone less low and less even . . . and then: "You're damn right they're tired, Ed. They're damn fucking tired! We're all tired! WE'VE BEEN HERE ALL FUCKING DAY DOING THIS SHIT AND WE CAN'T TAKE IT ANYMORE AND YOU ASK IF WE'RE TIRED?!"

Silence. A moment. Then . . .

John: "Sorry. I'm sorry. Um, let's continue." And John began to wheel himself on his podium over to the next set, leaving all of us a bit stunned. "All right," said John, calmly. "Let's take this from the top."

The actors began to speak their lines, and suddenly John slammed his fist onto his roly-podium. "I'm sorry—goddamnit, Ed.! You ask if we're tired? Tired?! I'VE NEVER, IN ALL MY YEARS, BEEN TREATED LIKE THIS. GODDAMNIT, ED.!" and he slammed his fist into the podium again.

Right about here, I realized that maybe I shouldn't be standing between John and Ed.

But again John calmed himself down. "Sorry. Sorry. Once more, please. Sorry." Nobody moved. John extended a handshake to Ed. and said, "Eddie . . . friend . . . sorry."

No one has ever called Ed. Weinberger "Eddie," ever. And "friend" was even stranger. John may as well have said "Kemo sabe."

"Okay," said John. "Let's continue. Please. From the top. Thank you."

The actors hesitantly began to speak again.

"NO!" screamed John, slamming the podium. "GODDAMNIT ED.! YOU SAID TIRED! TIRED?! I CAN'T FUCKING BELIEVE TIRED! TIRED!"

And he knocked his podium aside and stormed off, disappearing behind the set as thirty people stood, dumbfounded. Then, from behind the set, we heard *Crash!* Tables, chairs, craft service trays being flung and knocked about for several seconds—*Crash! Bang! Pow!* A door slammed . . . and silence. A beat, and then Ed. spoke for the first time. "Well," Ed. said in his soft, trademark whine, "he wasn't too tired to have three helpings of Chinese food tonight."

No showrunner has ever been banned from the sets of his own shows more than Ed. He inspired this kind of rage everywhere he went and yet was also able to defuse it instantly with a gorgeous fat joke. You had to love him.

Oliver and I worked on *Down the Shore* next. It was on Fox and it was the first show created by Alan Kirschenbaum. Three girls and three guys share a beach house at the Jersey Shore. In 1992, it was kind of a precursor to *Friends*, except we didn't have the *Friends.* It lasted twenty-six episodes over two seasons, and was replaced by *Whoops,* the sitcom about the only survivors of a nuclear holocaust.

We had a good time doing *Down the Shore,* but now it was time for Oliver and I to work on a show people had heard of. Alan was hired to run *Coach* (created by Barry Kemp), which was going into its sixth season, and he kindly took us with him. *Coach* was about a college football coach. There were two things I knew about football: One was that it was something the rest of the country was obsessed with, and the other was that the boys who played it in high school would knock my books down in the hall. Oliver knew even less about sports. We actually wrote in a script once, "That coach wouldn't know his (your football term here) from his (different football term here)."

About a year into our stint on *Coach,* we received an interesting phone call: Would we want to write a sitcom pilot for Peter O'Toole? I remember, very distinctly, saying, "Huh?" Why would Peter O' Toole, *Sir* Peter O'Toole, want to do a sitcom? Well, he had recently done a movie called *King Ralph* with John Goodman, where Goodman had turned him on to his excellent and very popular sitcom, *Roseanne.* He also introduced Mr. O'Toole to the concept of syndication. And so our phone rang.

Oliver and I very quickly and excitedly wrote a pilot script and sent it to O'Toole's people. The premise: Peter O'Toole would play a famous author who loses all his friends when he writes a tell-all tome—he's ostracized from his world. He shows up at the door of his estranged daughter, who is a single mom, a dental assistant raising a particularly nerdy thirteen-year-old boy. The show is about her trying to have a life while Lawrence of Arabia is in the kitchen.

Our phone rang again, and this time it was Mr. O'Toole himself calling us from London. "Is this Rosencrantz and Guildenstern?" he cheerily asked. "Call us whatever you like," I said. We talked for an hour. He was happy with the script and said we should get together in New York to talk some more.

Oliver and I flew to New York. We were waiting in a hotel room when the door flew open and in whisked the world's most charming person, scarf flowing behind him like a Bedouin robe. We spent the day with him—breakfast at Wolf's deli, lunch at the Oyster Bar at the Plaza, walking through the streets of midtown as New Yorkers gasped. It was *My Favorite Year* in a day. I'll never forget it.

O'Toole had notes on the script, and I never had better notes on anything, before or since. We went back to LA, made the script better, sent it off to him . . . and he agreed to do it. Peter O'Toole was on board. We hand in the script to the comedy people at NBC, who also like it. We start casting the other roles. It's very thrilling. And then the president of NBC says, "You know, I'd rather not have someone with an accent on the network." And the project was dead.

"Someone with an accent."

You have to hold your head at the exact right angle so your brains don't spill out your ears.

I'll tell you something: Peter O'Toole sitting in a chair talking to the camera about whatever the hell he wanted to talk about for an hour or two a week would be a gift to America.

We took the show to another network. And another. Nobody else wanted it, either—the accent was a problem, plus, O'Toole was sixty-two—not the desired demographic. I pause here to let you contemplate the nature of the television business, and the fate of our nation.

Oliver lasted two more seasons on *Coach* before striking out on his own; I stayed one more season, establishing myself as a solo writer; and Barry Kemp was kind enough to let me direct an episode.

That brings me to 1995. I was thirty-five, and I was starting to wonder if perhaps there wasn't a better way.

Professionally, after ten years as a struggling actor and five years as a sitcom writer, I was still looking for the same feeling I had had when I did shows for free in high school, or college, or summer stock. Money doesn't make a show better. In fact, I'd argue the opposite. I'd seen the face of big business television, and that face was Frank Fontaine's as the drunken barfly on *The Jackie Gleason Show*—all cross-eyed and weaving. "Hiya, Joe. Hello, Mr. Dunahee-hee-hee." Lunacy passing for reasonable business decisions. Too many shows my Oma referred to as "Kvatch mit souza" (Crap with sauce on it). I didn't understand the business then and I'm still constantly baffled by it now. My values had been established, and I didn't realize it, but all the experiences, and all the lessons from the various showrunners I had worked for were going to prove to be invaluable, as I was about to find myself in just such a position. I'll tell you the single best piece of advice I ever got from anyone about anything. It was from Ed. Weinberger. He said, "Do the show you want to do, because in the end, they're going to cancel you anyway."

4

How About This Guy?

There are a million reasons why a project—any project, in any field—can fail. In the world of television sitcom pilots, you could do a nice job, do everything right, and one cast member doesn't jive with the others . . . dead. A guy at the network has a bad day when deciding your fate, or they test the show in Las Vegas to teenagers, or the zeitgeist moves an inch to the right . . . dead.

When filming: Are you getting the reaction on camera?

Are you too far from the actors or too close?

Did you not hit exactly what's funniest about your premise, the timing of the editing, the lighting, the camera angles? Did you compromise the show by taking all the studio's and network's notes?

All these elements are conspiring to not be funny, and if they do, then . . . you're dead. There are a million ways for you to get it wrong, not to mention what other people do. How is it marketed? Are the audience's expectations going to be met by what it has been sold? Is it on the right evening around other shows that are compatible?

There are umpteen factors you can't control. So you have to make sure the ones you can control are so fantastic, they trump the ones you can't. Your show has to be undeniable. It makes for an enormous amount of pressure, but in 1995 I wasn't thinking about any of this. I was on *Coach.*

During my time on *Coach,* I rose to the rank of supervising producer. What does that mean? It means writer. It means writer who's been there a little longer than producer, or story editor, but not as long as co–executive producer or executive producer. In other words, those fancy-schmancy titles you see in the credits of TV shows all mean writer, and the schmancier the title, the more say that guy has in what we'll order for lunch.

I'm so glad someone mentioned lunch, because now we come to the writer's main preoccupation. When you're sitting in The Room with the same man-children, sometimes a mixed-up lady, assorted Silly Puttys, rubber balls, and a dictionary, and you're in there all day, every day, it can start to feel like what my ex-partner Oliver called The Veal Pen. And the only sunlight coming into that room is The Menu. Chinese, deli, Greek, sushi, Indian, anything you want, from any place in town. This alone is reason to work in television. An absolutely fantastic perk. So fantastic, I gained thirty pounds in five years. Monica didn't mind. She loved me anyway—she never cared about looks. She sees what's beautiful inside a person. And so I rewarded that nice trait of hers by becoming a fat load.

What I could do for my wife now, though, was buy her a little house. We had moved out of Patti's, and lived in an apartment on Beachwood Canyon Drive under the Hollywood sign for five years, saving the TV money. This was the same building Alan Kirschenbaum lived in, with the same couch I slept on when I first arrived, and soon other friends—actors, writers—started renting in the building, until it felt like a dorm. I remember walking down the hall in my socks to Alan's apartment to play this new thing he got called Nintendo. Hours of fun times. We were idiots. Some sitcom writing buddies and comedians would meet down the street at Victor's Deli every Sunday for lunch, and fifteen years later, we still do. Great food and wonderful service . . . maybe I'll get a free sandwich.

So, a house. We had saved up our money and we were looking to buy a little house with a big East Coast pine tree out front we loved in Los Feliz, a beautiful, East Coast–type neighborhood with nice houses and lawns. I told the Realtor a price that I couldn't go above, but the seller kept asking for more, kept jacking it up. You know this game? Your Realtor, as soon as you pick the house, actually starts working against you, trying to get the price up so her commission goes up. I would say, "Okay, I agree to that price." And the Realtor would say, "Well, they want more, there's another offer."

"Oh, okay. I'll go up a little higher."

But then I reached this point where she had done this to me five times. I finally said, "I can't go any higher, that's it." She said, "Well, you better go higher because there's another offer." I said, "Well, I guess we'll have to give it to them, then. What can I do? Good-bye." And I hung up.

And Monica said, "Why are you sad?" And I said, "I think we lost the house today."

And she started crying. We've lost our house. The next day the phone rang. The Realtor said, "They're going to let you have the house for the price you wanted."

"Wow," I said. "Why?"

She said, "They like you better than the other couple."

"Really?" I said. "Is that because we're not fictional?"

So we moved into the house with the pine tree and had a baby boy named Ben. Sweetest boy in the whole world, I love him to death, changed my life. If you haven't had a kid yet, go have one. I'll wait.

It's May 1995. Monica and I are in bed. Nothing's going on (relax), so we're watching *Letterman.* And here comes a comedian. We always root for the comedian, because we enjoy the comedy and we know the pressure the comedian must be under. To even get the shot on Letterman's show, like Johnny Carson's before him, is a once-in-a-lifetime opportunity. Monica's pretty empathetic anyway—she tells a story of watching *The Tonight Show* once when they had a bird on, which was going to break an egg by throwing a rock at it with its beak. Well, the bird kept missing the egg, and missing, and missing, as Johnny stood by, and my wife got a stomachache. Monica felt bad for the bird. "It's so awkward. The bird must be embarrassed. I just feel terrible," she said.

Okay, so we're watching *Letterman,* and here comes a new comedian, first time on the show . . . and he's funny. He's doing well. He talks about his twin baby boys and how he hasn't written any new material since they were born except . . . "Well, here's the one new joke I've written," he says. "Tell me if you like this." And he pulls out a ring of keys, and shakes it out in front of him. "Here you go. Look! Look!" We crack up. "I'm glad you liked that," he says to the audience. "Otherwise I'd have to come down and rub my nose in your bellies."

So we like that guy . . . and we go to sleep. And naturally, forget about him.

Three months go by. Life goes on. I work on *Coach.* We play with our boy. A videotape shows up at the house. It's this comedian's appearance on *Letterman,* the same show we saw. It turns out that he had been a stand-up for twelve years before getting his shot on *Letterman,* and from that one six-minute appearance, David Letterman said, "There should be a show for this guy." So they started sending this tape around looking for writers who might want to create a show for this Ray Romano fellow.

That's how it works sometimes: You get tapes of actors and comedians, and your writing samples are being sent to actors and comedians who are looking for writers. If you have a meeting, and it works out, maybe you get paid to write a pilot script. So sure, I'll take this meeting—Ray's act is relatable. He comes across as a down-to-earth guy, and he talks about his kids—just like Cosby did—and Cosby was always one of my favorites.

Ray and I met at Art's Deli on Ventura Boulevard, "where every sandwich is a work of Art." I didn't write that—that's on their calendar. And we just hit it off. He was born in Queens; I was born in Queens. He likes Cosby, too. He has a crazy Italian family; I have a facachta Jewish family, not such a big difference. In both all problems are solved with food, and the mother never leaves you alone. For every story he had about his family, I had one, too. What I liked about him instantly was how unassuming, to the point of neurotic, he seemed to be. He was nervous about Hollywood, and seemed nervous about people in general. I couldn't let him know at the time that I was pretty much the same way—I was supposed to instill trust in me. I think he met with a dozen other guys, and I was not his first choice, but I got lucky. The other guy was from a new hot show, *Friends*, but he was busy. So I get the call. They want to know if I can go to New York now and meet with David Letterman.

Great. I go to New York, to the Ed Sullivan Theater, and go upstairs. It was after a show. Mr. Letterman was just done taping for the evening, and they had me go to his office. At the doorway, there's David Letterman, postshow, in sweat clothes, sneakers, baseball hat, cigar. Hello, very nice. Now, when you go into his office, the desk is facing the wrong way. You come in and you're behind his desk. That's weird, right? Oh, by the way, heavy metal music is playing loudly on his stereo. And they don't shut it off for the meeting. It's really very loud. Mr. Letterman says, "Have a seat." And he gestures for me to sit behind the desk. I say, "Not behind the desk." He says, "Absolutely, behind the desk." So I sit behind the desk, and he and two of his producers sit across from me in chairs. Like it's my office and my meeting. The first thing I do is tell them to get the hell out of my office.

What was nice about it was they treated me as if I had the job already. They were very cordial to me. They asked me if I had thought about what the premise of the show would be. I really hadn't yet, but I did think that at the center would be Ray's persona. "He seems to be the show," I said. Pretty lame, no? I guess that wasn't such a terrible answer.

The one piece of advice that Letterman gave me—I'll never forget it, very encouraging—was: "Don't embarrass us." And I didn't realize it then, but that was the job interview. I couldn't hear half of it because of the heavy metal music, but I guess it went well enough. The show, if we could sell it, was to be a coproduction of Letterman's company (World Wide Pants) and HBO Independent Productions, two very small production companies joining forces, and the next stop was for me to pitch an idea for this thing at CBS. So now is the time when I have to really figure out what this show with this Ray Romano is going to be. I talk to Ray. I'm going to make sure he's on board with whatever we're going to do, then I'll pitch it to CBS with him next to me (if you can go in with a star, you do). And if they buy it, I'll go write the pilot script. We met at my house and we were talking, just socially, as you would when you're going to work with someone. We didn't sing "Getting to Know You," we had lunch, and we talked some more about his life and where he's from.

Ray said, "Well, I live in Queens and I've got this family—twin boys and an older daughter and my parents live close by. They live with my older brother who's a police sergeant who eats every bite of food like this, touches it to his chin before he eats it. And he's kind of jealous of me even though he's older and he's a cop. Like he came over one day and saw my Cable Ace award for stand-up, and he goes, 'It never ends for Raymond. Ehhhverybody loves Raymond.' "

And I said, "Well, it doesn't sound like there's anything there we could use."

No, really—I knew that was the show. What else should it be? First of all, Ray had never acted before. I wasn't going to make him a gay astronaut from Cleveland. He had to be comfortable, as comfortable as he could be while being on television. So surround him with his own life. Ray actually wasn't so sure. Nobody really thinks his own stupid life is worth watching. Besides, he wanted to do more of a *Seinfeld* type of show anyway—he and his friends sitting in the diner, talking and making jokes. But in 1995, there was a lot of that kind of thing already on the air. Larry David and his writers and cast on *Seinfeld* did what they did brilliantly. I always thought that the only thing wrong with *Seinfeld* was all the shows that were trying to imitate it. And there were so many imitations we were getting, and still are—Xeroxes of Xeroxes.

Besides, if this was going to be the first show I ever created, I should write what I was comfortable with, the kind of show I knew best and loved, in the style of classic, old-fashioned types of shows, like *The Honeymooners, Dick Van Dyke, All in the Family, Mary Tyler Moore, The Odd Couple, Taxi.* Shows that didn't depend on topical jokes, or the social rituals and foibles of the day, shows where the humor came from character, where the story came from character, and there was a story—beginning, middle, and end.

One of the popular myths about *Seinfeld* was that it was about nothing. Bullshit. The shows that imitated it bought that myth and so *they* were about nothing. *Seinfeld* was first and foremost about those four characters and a very specific viewpoint about life. No one would have watched if it really was about nothing. So I wanted this show with Raymond to be about something. I wanted, since I might not get to have this opportunity again, to try to make something that would have lasting value. Why build something temporary? I looked at my TV and saw it cluttered up with disposable entertainment. Not even entertainment, but what I called the illusion of entertainment: sets and costumes, hairstyles, actors, shoes, nipples, all flashing before our faces with MTV-style editing, so fast and so much that at the end of a half hour, you think you were entertained. No content. No time for content. "We're moving—next!" I thought maybe our show would stand out if we went the other way. And so, armed with this idea and Ray Romano, I went into Les Moonves's new presidential office at CBS and told them what I planned.

Now, CBS, they're in the business of doing big things to get people to watch. And so I can tell you that they certainly were not jumping up and down for this show. They were not saying, "We have to do this. It sounds so exciting. A guy who lives across the street from his parents."

I couldn't blame them. Who was I? Nobody. And the star I walked in with was sitting there, shlumped on the couch. He looked as though he'd be happier if nobody noticed him and he could pocket some of the hard candy off of Mr. Moonves's coffee table. And yes, we didn't walk into the room with what they call a high concept. But they did like Ray's stand-up, and I told them that his actual, real life was even better. And what I didn't know about his life, or the personalities of his family, I'd fill in with the details of my own life, and the characters in my family.

It also didn't hurt that we came from David Letterman, whom CBS had a development deal with, and always liked to keep happy.

But this was Mr. Moonves's first year as president of CBS, and I was told he wanted high-profile shows with big stars. What chance did we have?

Okay, if this chapter was a sitcom episode, that last question would be what The Room calls schmuck bait. Schmuck bait is a gambit in the story that the audience knows can't possibly happen, like "Uh-oh, the bus is going off a cliff and the whole cast might die in the pilot." You can only bait a schmuck with such a plot point, because the audience knows there's no show if that happens, and it's the end of television.

And still I say, "What chance did we have?" to you!

Sorry for yelling, but really, I know it is a foregone conclusion that they picked the show up, and it became the show we know. But it was a miracle that such a big corporation would say yes to this idea. And that it would let me go write the script. And that the casting worked out, and then everything else happened that got us on the air. And then to survive a few episodes. And then a whole season. And then another season. And then to have any success beyond that at all. All the planets have to line up, and God has to stop what he's doing and say, "Okay, you people with the TV show on Channel 2 with the arguing, you get to live your dream."

So that December afternoon in 1995, we sold the show.

I had a wonderful moment of happiness, followed immediately by an oy. My mind flooded with the million things that could go wrong. Starting with the script I now had to write.

5

Always Quit

I've learned that if good fortune should smile on you, you should take a moment to acknowledge it and recognize that you're entitled to some happiness in your life, but most important, you shouldn't celebrate prematurely. A guy and his wife invited us out to a dinner party once and everything was going along nicely, good food, wine, people, and then he clinked his glass with his fork, stood up in the restaurant, and addressed us. "Something exciting happened today. We spoke to a really rich billionaire type of guy, and he's going to meet with us about the possibility of investing in our company." And then he stood there and waited for us to congratulate him on the *meeting* about the *possibility.* Of course what ultimately happened to this gentleman was like the fate of the actor at the Hitler auditions in *The Producers,* where he proudly exclaims, "And I was recently up for the lead in the Broadway production of *The Gypsy Lover.*"

"What happened?"

"I didn't get it."

When the network makes the commitment to you to go forward

with the writing of the pilot script, this aspiring Hitler scene should be playing in the back of your head. The network commissions more than fifty pilot scripts a year and shoots maybe a dozen. Be encouraged, but don't throw the dinner party just yet with the clinking and the standing.

The first thing the person assigned to cover our show for the network wanted to know was what the pilot episode's plot was going to be. So right away, annoyingly, work is involved. I have an idea—Ray's wife tells him that he's on the road too much and she's stuck all the time, not just in the house with the kids, but with his family across the street. Ray says he'd love to help out more, but as a sportswriter he has to travel, she knows this. Finally, to appease the wife, Ray agrees to talk to his boss, knowing full well nothing can be done. Ray talks to his boss, and to his unhappy surprise, Ray's boss tells him that with the new satellite dishes, he doesn't have to travel quite as much. He can stay home more and still cover the games. That's the first act.

The second act is Ray at home, trying to work, dealing with the family, and that way we get to know all our characters and establish the situation. Okay? Very nice.

The network guy hated this idea. "Too premisey," he said. The networks don't like what's called a premise pilot—one where the premise of the series is established—because it's not indicative of what the other episodes will be like. They want an episode that could be episode number two or twelve or thirty. But sometimes it's very necessary to establish how the sit part of the sitcom came to be. How will the audience understand a story without a beginning? I also didn't feel that this story was even that premisey—premisey would have been the day Ray and Debra moved in across the street from his parents (a show we saved for our first end-of-the-year flashback). But you have to pick your fights, and this wasn't such a big one yet. So I pocketed this idea (eventually using it in season two) and came up with another idea for that first story. And, as required, I had to run it by the studio people before it could go to the network people. I had two studios on this show, and everyone had to agree. It's too boring to tell you this next idea. Suffice it to say that after the studios changed it out of fear that it, too, would be too premisey for the network, it became terribley. The network guy rejected that one, too, and then another one that had been picked over and changed by the studio people. As the network guy rejected that third idea he said to me, "I'm beginning to think that maybe you can't do this."

Maybe I couldn't. Maybe this was going to be like waiting two hours on line for Space Mountain only to have your seven-year-old son say as they're strapping both of you in, "I'm not doing this." And the ride is over.

No. I decided to quickly let this guy know he could trust me to write this pilot. I thought of a very simple story and called him back directly. "It's Debra's birthday and she would rather celebrate it with just Ray and the kids this year, without his family coming over."

"That's it," said Network Guy. "Go write it."

I then had to call the studios and let them know we were now okay, and they were relieved and somewhat surprised. But at least we were in business, and that's all they really cared about.

Next step in the process is the outline—about five to seven pages of just the story. I ran it by Ray, and then got it approved by the studio people (not without a nasty insight into someone's character, which we'll discuss later), then the outline was approved by the network, and then I could go on to write the script.

The hard part was over for me—coming up with the story, which is also the most important part. That's what makes or breaks an episode, a movie, a play, a book, anything where *a story is being told.* Why not have a good story, good characters, make it mean something for the long, not the short, term? This was my shot. I wanted the pilot episode of this series to stand out. I wanted the show to be about family, to have stories that came from character, for the characters and the situations they were in to be funny and relatable. I thought about the movies I'd loved. How many times had I gone to the movies lately and left feeling ripped off? And it's only gotten worse. I always feel it is as if the work stopped with the poster. "Hey, Will Ferrell as a Genie with a dog." Calculate the first weekend's grosses, take a picture, make the poster, shoot the trailer, fill the movie with crap. "We scammed 'em again." There's no character detail, no specificity, nobody cares, here's a poop joke: "The twist is Will poops *on the dog.*" The whole culture seems to be living for instant reactions. The media, even our government's motto seems to be: Get It Now, Screw Later. We're inside a disposable, tabloid, celebrity-driven world, that's rapidly draining our heads, and filling it with so-called entertainment that has the shelf life of an ice cube on the radiator. I pause now, to drink some scotch.

So the question the Powers That Be were asking in 1996 was: How will this Raymond show stand out? It'll stand out by being half decent, that's how. I never said that to anyone, but it was how I psyched myself up. To keep from throwing up.

Time to write. Okay. Time to write. Here we go. Any minute now, we're writing and it'll be good. To be writing. Love writing. Here it comes. AAAAALL the writing.

I suck at writing.

Here's a little insight about "the process." I don't think worrying is necessarily a bad thing. Maybe shows and movies and the quality of a lot of other things would be better if people worried about them a little more . . . is what I told myself to stop from worrying about worrying. Here was my biggest worry: What did I have that the other sitcom writers didn't? I had the very funny Ray and his family, but I didn't really know them. And then I realized what I had: I had my own experience.

I had my wife. I had my parents. I had the Fruit-of-the-Month Club story.

If that story hadn't gotten some laughs from the guests at my brother's wedding, I might not have had the confidence to put it into the script. It just happened to be a pretty good, economical illustration of how nuts "Ray's" parents were, and what Ray and Debra were going to be up against across the street.

But the key was that specificity. I didn't know it then, but I learned that this was the universal element. If I had tried to hit everybody with a vague example, I would've missed everybody. What I stumbled onto was that each of our lives deals in specifics, and we relate to that specificity in other people's lives. For example, people still tell me that they can't give a gift to their parents without it blowing up in their faces. And, even crazier, they've had that exact experience with their parents and the Fruit-of-the-Month Club. So I'm very happy that so many people are out of their minds, and we can all laugh, or cry, together.

That story served as the second act complication in the script, where Ray comes over to lie to his parents about why they won't all be celebrating Debra's birthday together this year. He says that he's taking Debra and the kids to Bear Mountain (which is close to where I grew up in Rockland), but before he can get to that lie, the fruit tragedy lets us know this isn't going to be easy for Raymond. Ever.

Other details from our actual lives were also liberally sprinkled around that pilot script—Ray's father really did change the outgoing message on Ray and his wife, Anna's, answering machine, causing Anna, in real life, to cry.

Ray's father also enjoyed sniffing the heads of babies, claiming he could "suck in their youth." Ray's brother, Richard, on whom Robert is loosely based, actually has the habit of touching food to his chin before eating it, and really did say in a jealous moment, "It never ends for Raymond. Everybody loves Raymond."

My wife and I occasionally speak to each other in a manner reminiscent of the way Ray and Debra speak to each other. And so do Ray and Anna, and, happily, so do you and your whoever.

The rest of the story—the situation, dialogue, other character traits, and relationships—were made up, but the point is, I had enough real life in there to make it feel like real life. And in January 1996, when I was about to hand in the pilot script, I thought it might also be funny. But I certainly wasn't sure, so I sent my first draft to Jeremy Stevens. Jeremy is about twenty years older than I and has a great eye and ear. He was one of the creators of *The Electric Company,* he worked on *Fernwood 2-Night* and *Saturday Night Live,* and we were army buddies. By "army" I mean we had both survived *Baby Talk.* But I wasn't sending Jeremy the script because of his impressive credentials; I was sending him the first pilot script I ever wrote on my own because he was the sweetest guy I knew. Whatever he had to say, he'd at least say it nicely. Jeremy didn't disappoint.

The first words I heard from him when I picked up the phone were: "We'll be on for ten years!" He was very excited.

It turns out he was wrong, we were only on for nine years, but I'll never forget his enthusiasm and friendship (he's not dead, I just appreciate him), which sustained me over some of the rough times to come.

The network liked the script enough to call the pilot a go but of course that implied a casting contingent go, which means it wasn't a go unless we could find a cast the network would approve. So I was assigned a casting director, Lisa Miller, and she started bringing me people to see as if I was a producer.

The Brother

Ray's real brother, Richard the police sergeant, is shorter than Ray, so naturally we started looking for a shorter fellow to play Robert—the older brother who would literally have to look up to Raymond. And then this talking tree came into the casting office. His name was Brad Garrett, and when he walked in I thought, *Well . . . here's another way to go. . . .* When he opened his mouth, and those basso profundo notes came out with brilliant timing, matchless facial expression, and expert delivery, I fell over laughing. This was nothing like Ray's or my life; it was better. That was easy. We found the brother.

The Father

The network approved Brad right away, but we started hearing about how we shouldn't go too ethnic with the cast. What does that mean? It means that for this show to play in Middle America, we couldn't have too many overtly swarthy Italian or Jewish types populating this family. Ray and Brad are both, and respectively, swarthy, Italian, and Jewish.

I asked, "It's an Italian family. What are we supposed to cast?" Network Guy says, "Nonethnic ethnic."

This was a new concept to me. But I soon realized what they meant because Les Moonves provided the perfect example of the nonethnic ethnic when he suggested Peter Boyle for the role of Frank Barone. Peter Boyle says New York ethnic without saying Italian or Jewish. Peter Boyle is decidedly Irish, which I've come to understand means nonethnic ethnic. We've come a long way.

Peter Boyle showed up for our meeting an hour late. He got bad directions on the lot and was sent on a wild goose chase on a very hot day trying to find us. When he finally did, he was pissed off. Now, I only know this man from seeing him in *Young Frankenstein* and, worse, *Joe.* Joe shot punks like me for fun, and here he comes into the room, angry at me. At that moment, he wasn't a movie star to me, he was a big, angry movie star. He scared me, and I gave him the part.

He happened to be funny, too, when he calmed down. But we also saw that we could use a little of that anger. The truth is, Peter is a sweetheart, a liberal, and has led one of the more interesting lives on the planet. Here are two things I was stunned to learn: He had been a monk, and John Lennon was the best man at Peter's wedding.

Lucky for us, he also was hilarious at sitting in a chair with his pants open and rifling off one-liners at his wife, his sons, and anyone else in range. We had the father.

The Mother

I saw more than a hundred women for this role in New York and Los Angeles. It was very tough for me to cast, because I had someone very specific in mind for this mother . . . my mother. And she was too ethnic.

Doris Roberts came into the room, a fifty-year veteran of stage and screen, read the Fruit-of-the-Month scene, and was perfect. She doesn't look anything like my mother, but she just totally got what was in my head and in my life. She also has perfect timing, delivery, and facial expression. There was no runner-up. It seemed as if she was born to do this role. I was starting to feel lucky. It was starting to look a lot like a show.

The Wife

The wife in a sitcom is the hardest part to cast. She can't just be the straight man or the nice lady who says, "Here's your lunch, honey." She has to be all things to all people: funny, tough, sexy, sweet, vulnerable, confident, charming. I'm lucky because I found her in real life, too.

I didn't marry that girl . . .

But I know where she is.

Wife joke. Half the jokes on *Raymond* were wife jokes. The other half were husband jokes.

The week we start casting, I get a call from Network Guy, who asks me, "Who are you casting for the wife?" I say, "Honestly, I'm looking now. I'm looking all over the place." (I think ultimately I saw two hundred women for that part in New York and LA, flying back and forth.) He says, "Well, Les Moonves wants this one actress [we'll call her So-and-So]. So you should cast her." I say, "Oh, but I think she's completely wrong." He says, "You didn't hear me. Les wants her. If you don't cast her, you don't have a show." End of discussion. This is exactly what I had been waiting for—the end of my luck.

I call my agent, and I say, "Can you believe this? They're making me take this actress. . . . This So-and-So is horrible for the part. She's won't be funny in this. They only want her because she's a blonde. She's wispy. She's waspy. She's totally, completely wrong for the show and will ruin the whole thing. What do I do?" And my agent says, "I would cast her."

And I say, "No. In fact, I quit. Tell them I quit." He goes, "Don't be an idiot. If you don't take her, you're not going to have a show." I say, "I don't have a show *with* her. I'm an idiot if I do this because I'm killing the whole thing if I cast So-and-So. And I already have a blonde—Doris Roberts." He says, "Well, why don't you let So-and-So read for you?" I say, "You're right. Yes." Listen, I would love to be wrong and then have a show, right? I tell my agent to please have her come in. But . . . she won't read. Why? Because she's So-and-So. I say, "Will she meet with me?" My agent calls her people. They say yes. So I meet with So-and-So. It's the morning I'm going to bring my three actress choices into the network. The way this works is you bring them in one at a time, and they all audition for the same part, and then they leave the room. And what they told me was going to happen was, Les Moonves would then stand up and say, "What about So-and-So?" And if you don't say, "I'm going to cast her," you're dead. Okay?

So I'm very nervous this morning. It's the morning I have to meet with So-and-So, and that afternoon I have to go to the network with my three actresses. By the way, Patty Heaton is not one of them. I hadn't found her yet. I didn't even know she existed yet. But I did have three decent choices, certainly better for the role than So-and-So.

So I meet with So-and-So, and she's very nice. Lovely, pretty. And during the meeting I kind of talk her into reading. And she reads for me . . . and she's ten times worse than I thought she would be for this part. So now I'm crying, because this is the day I lose my show because I cannot do it. I cannot. We go to the CBS offices, I have a bowling ball in my stomach, my three actresses read, they leave, and Les Moonves, right on cue, stands up and goes, "What about So-and-So?"

I say, "I love her. I think she's great. I've loved her in everything she's done. And I met with her today, and she's beautiful and charming, and I fell in love with her. I wanted to marry her. But then she read for me, and I have to tell you, it's just not what I wrote. You know? I don't really buy them as a couple. Could she do it? . . . Maybe. But I also think, maybe, we could do better." And Les Moonves shrugs and says, "It was just an idea."

I learned a big lesson that day. First of all, what do you think really happened at CBS when the So-and-So idea first came up? Probably what happened was, there was a meeting, and Les Moonves has many, many meetings about many, many things, and the casting of this little sitcom with no stars in it comes up, and he says, "What about So-and-So for the wife?" And Mr. Network Guy thinks, *I'll be the one to get him So-and-So and I'll tell him I was the one and then I'll be getting a promotion.* . . . Instead, he was fired two weeks later. I learned that just because they tell you, "The boss wants So-and So," there might be other agendas. And also, I was somewhat diplomatic and deferential to the king, which it's always good to be. A week later, Patty Heaton walked into our office, was perfect, met every quality I mentioned at the beginning of this chapter and then some, and was cast. That simple. When it's right, it's right, and now we could go film a show.

Not time to celebrate yet; if the network shoots about twelve comedy pilots a year, only about four make it onto television. Sometimes two.

The production week of the pilot shoot went pretty smoothly. The cast gathered at my house the day before production started for a get-acquainted brunch and read-through of the script. They were hilarious together. The next day we had the official table reading, and then I went into a room to get notes from the studio and the network. Here is my favorite note from that day: "I noticed that at the end of this episode, Ray tells his parents that maybe they shouldn't come over so much anymore."

"Yes?" I said.

"Well, my question is, if Ray says that to his parents, what happens in next week's episode if he's told them not to come over anymore?"

I paused to really understand this question. "Well . . . just off the top of my head . . . they don't listen to him."

During rehearsals that week, I noticed that maybe Brad had a little too much of a bitter edge to Robert. So I talked to him about it. I said, "Maybe Robert is a little more resigned to his lot in life, more of a sad sack than a bitter guy. More like . . ."

And Brad said, "Like Eeyore?"

And I said, "Yes! Yes! That's the perfect image for Robert—Eeyore! That's hysterical—"

He said, "I *am* Eeyore."

"What?"

"I'm Eeyore. I do the voice of Eeyore in the *Winnie-the-Pooh* cartoons."

So I told him to please keep doing that.

Okay, so at the end of that week we filmed the pilot. The cast was sharp, the scenes seemed to work, the audience laughed. Most of them had never seen Raymond before that night, and they liked him, if not loved him, immediately. I thought we were in good shape. Now comes the testing.

There are testing facilities throughout the United States, and this particular one is in Glendale, California, an LA suburb. You stand behind a one-way mirror and watch people watch your show. Who is watching? About twenty people of various shapes and sizes—ten men and ten women. The only thing they have in common is that they think it's a good idea to take forty dollars from a stranger to come into a room and watch something. They come in and they sit in front of a TV, and then they are each handed a dial—turn it to the left anytime you don't like something, turn it to the right every time you do—*for every moment of the show.*

Which could bring up the question: *Who the hell watches TV this way*?

You'd think I'd be worried, but I have to admit, I wasn't very nervous—even though this was my first exposure to this process and my fate hung in their knobs. But not only did I find it ridiculous, I had already seen the show work in front of the audience that was there the night we filmed it—and so did everyone else who now had to "test" it.

The show begins playing for these layabouts, and they start turning their dials. We can see an actual electronic recording of their responses as they happen, and here's what it looks like: Whenever there's a set-up, or a straight line, the dial gets turned to the left, and for every joke that's uttered it gets turned to the right. When someone they recognize comes in the door, a turn to the right. "Hey, who's that?" A turn to the left . . . until the new person says a joke . . . and then a turn to the right. A dramatic moment shows as a flatline, as if everyone in the testing room has died, open-mouthed, literally not knowing which way to turn. My God, won't someone help these people?

Lives are changed on these findings.

One rather large gentleman wasn't turning his dial at all. That's because he was asleep. This might've scared the hell out of me if he hadn't fallen asleep as soon as the lights went out. Forty dollars, air-conditioning, a comfy chair. It's a living.

The next thing the executives get for their forty dollars apiece is the men go into one room and the women go into another to discuss what they've just seen with a moderator. We get to watch and listen behind the glass for this portion, too. I know everything could have come crashing down (the show, not the glass, although wouldn't that be great?), but I was kind of enjoying this whole thing. Look at all the people, and the technology, and the time being devoted to the show. As stupid as this process is, I was flattered.

One fellow, a British man with an accent not unlike Eliza Doolittle's father's, summed up our show thusly: "I think Ray's a wimp, and I hate all these shows about wimps, and Ray's a real big wimp, and I wouldn't watch this show unless my wife forced me."

Just then a little fight broke out in the ladies' discussion group: One young woman didn't like the Marie character. "She's exactly like my mother-in-law, a real pain in the ass." And an older lady said, "She's just trying to help. She's a mother." And they went at it, not unlike Marie and Debra. And as the moderator tried to steer them back to the subject of scoring the pilot episode, I had a cookie.

A couple of Sundays later, I was at Victor's with my friends when Bill Gotti, the owner, came over and said, "There's a call for you by the register. It's Les Moonves."

"Whoooah," said my friends as I got up to get the phone.

"What, I'm eating," I said as my little joke to the Head of Everything.

And Les said, "Order an ice cream sundae."

What a nice way to hear good news. This was the best thing to happen to me in a deli since the old lady wanted me in bed with her dogs. I walked back over to the table and said, "I guess I'm buying lunch."

So the test scores were good enough to get picked up. Not great, but not terrible, like the test numbers for that bomb *Seinfeld.* I got a call from my agent, who had also just heard the news. "Congratulations," he said. "It's so great they're picking up the show."

I said, "Mazel tov, now we can celebrate."

He said, "They want to know who's going to run it."

I said, "What?"

"Who's going to run the show?"

"Call me crazy, but I assumed . . . me."

He said, "You? You've never run a show before." (The showrunner is responsible for every creative decision on the show—he's the Boss.)

I said, "Well, they liked the pilot enough to pick up the show, right?"

"Yes."

"So we'll do more like that."

He said, "You don't get it. They're not going to take a chance on you. This is now a multimillion-dollar investment for them. They're not going to trust you with this."

And I said, "Well, I'm very upset. I'm certainly not going to work for someone else *on my own show.*"

He said, "What else can you do?"

I said, "I quit."

He said, "All right, don't get excited. I'll call you back."

He calls me back. He says, "Here's what they'll do; they'll bring in another showrunner with you, one that's had experience, then you can do it with him, as coshowrunners."

I said, "Oh, well, since you put it that way, I quit."

Because I know what'll happen. I'd still be working for that guy. All the decisions would be made by the guy who's done this before regardless of whether it's my show or not. So I quit. "Tell them I quit. Good-bye. Don't call me again." I hung up.

My wife looked at me. "What's the matter?"

"Put the champagne away."

For two days I sat. I heard nothing. They were going ahead with my show, without me. I got a call two days later from my agent. "Les is going to let you run the show."

"What? Myself?"

"Yes."

"Wow," I said. This was amazing news, out of the blue.

I asked, "Why?"

And my agent said, "He liked how you handled that thing with So-and-So."

6

A Snake in the Grass

I could've called this chapter "The First Season," but would you have been as excited? Don't worry, there really is a snake in the grass coming, but let's start at a nice place, Carnegie Hall, May 1996. We're at the upfronts—the events where the networks announce their new fall schedules to the advertisers and the press amid hoopla and shrimp. Les Moonves, in his first programming year as head of the network, had scheduled four new comedies: the new *Cosby* show, Ted Danson and Mary Steenburgen in *Ink,* Rhea Pearlman and Malcolm McDowell in *Pearl,* and our little wooden show. I got to sit in Carnegie Hall next to my father as they showed clips from the show, the two thousand people there laughed, and then Ray came out and did some hilarious stand-up, and introduced me in the audience. My dad was kvelling. For those of you who don't speak Yiddish, "kvelling" means what your dad does when his son and his son's new television show are introduced at Carnegie Hall. My father has a very expressive face—he looks like Phil Silvers meets William Frawley (Fred Mertz), and to see that face lit up in the theater like that . . . the feelings go back to birth, don't they? No matter how crazy the parents become.

Okay, the snake in the grass. We need to go back a bit . . . the morning after I got the job to write the pilot, there was a breakfast meeting at a hotel in New York—people from the two studios that produced the show were there, as well as Ray, his manager, and me. We're having a nice breakfast, and Ray excuses himself momentarily and leaves the table. The second Ray leaves, one of the studio people—let's call him Iago—leans over to me and says, "Just so you know, this is Ray's show."

"Excuse me?"

"It's Ray's show. Ray's the one we're backing. When push comes to shove, we'll always side with Ray. Just so you know."

Well, I thought, this was unusual breakfast conversation . . . especially seeing as how I had just started and there hadn't even been time for contention yet.

But this was the first red flag. Over the coming year, Iago would go on to try to drive a wedge between Ray and me, in an attempt to get my job for himself. Sounds crazy, no? Our existence was as shaky as . . . as . . . as a fiddler on the roof!

Among the many things Ray and I had in common were a certain Queens, New York, pessimism, skepticism, self-criticism. Ray had always written for himself; he's one of the best stand-up comedians in the country, and his material is terrific. To let someone else write for him would be an adjustment. Coming from sitcoms as I did, I think it's fair to say that Ray was understandably worried about a certain "hack factor," or "sitcommy-ness" that would be imposed upon him by me or any other sitcom writer in my position. Now the last thing I wanted to produce was a hacky sitcom, but Ray didn't know me or my high-falutin' values yet. He was in a new world, and nervous. Iago made sure to exploit these feelings. Why? Iago was unhappy where he was and would rather have run a show, especially a show that was a show already.

The next red flag was . . . redder.

I mentioned in the last chapter a certain nasty character insight I observed when I handed in my pilot outline. Again, the outline is the story of the episode, about six or seven pages long. You don't want too many people seeing this stage of the game because they're seeing you, the writer, half-dressed. You'll make a better impression when the dialogue is filled in, and it actually reads like a script, instead of a somewhat drier story. With that in mind, I handed in my outline for approval to two, and only two, people—one at each of the studios, and in large letters on a cover page, I wrote, "FOR YOUR EYES ONLY." I was nervous and sensitive about this, the first pilot story I had written alone. A couple of days later, I learned that Iago had photocopied my outline, distributed it to everyone involved in the production, including all the powers above us—Les Moonves, David Letterman, and Chris Albrecht (the head of HBO)—and stapled four pages of his notes to the outline.

I pause here so I can throw up again.

Whether the notes were valid or not valid is not the point (they were not valid). The point is that it was now obvious that Iago had an agenda. I called him.

"Why did you do that?" I asked in disbelief. "It said 'FOR YOUR EYES ONLY' on there."

"Phil, I don't know why you're getting so upset," he responded, reptilian-like.

"You really don't understand this? You're a writer!"

"Phil. We're all just trying to work together."

I don't need to go on. This was unpleasant for me. It continued to be somewhat unpleasant through the scriptwriting process, because Iago's notes (which he kept pumping into Ray's ears) were always, "There should be more Ray." He would have Ray ask me if there always needed to be a story, and couldn't Ray just sit in the diner with his friends and talk about funny things and why couldn't that be the show?

What was pleasant was that we got picked up for series anyway. We did get CBS's worst time slot (Friday at eight-thirty—there hadn't been a hit there since *Gomer Pyle*), but we got on because Les Moonves and his people at CBS (Wendi Trilling and Gene Stein) liked the show, and the testing wasn't terrible.

Since I was a first-time showrunner, my deal was low. In fact, I was the lowest-paid guy in town who was running a network show. What the network and studios did agree to in lieu of a fair salary, and betting with the odds that most shows don't make it, was a larger piece than normal of the show's profits for me—a percentage of the back end, or syndication, in the unlikely event we should be so lucky. I was fine with that. I'm not trying to be glib—at that time it was a risk, but I believed in the show. I loved it—I loved the actors, I loved the subject matter, I loved that I was getting a chance to write about my personal life, my family, and how I felt about stuff that mattered. I would've done this show for free. I'm not kidding. To have my own comedy on television was almost as good a feeling as getting the lead in the high school play. We had a couple of months before starting production, so the next thing I needed to do was find a writing staff. You can't write every episode yourself unless you're Aaron Sorkin, and he didn't need as many jokes in *The West Wing.* The phone started ringing off the hook with agents who wanted to send me "only their top five" clients' material. Like an idiot I'd say okay. Scripts from every agency in the land began to flood into my house, piling up in every corner, creating a fire hazard. Here's who I picked:

Jeremy Stevens. I told you about him.

Lew Schneider. Lew and I had been friends since *Down the Shore.* He was an actor in the show and went on to be a writer. He's also one of the funniest people in the world, and a great stand-up comedian, too. Some of his "Room bits" include making love to the thermostat. (Also to the table, also to Steve Skrovan).

Steve Skrovan. Another stand-up comedian, also turned writer (*Seinfeld*), also very funny, especially when being fornicated by Lew Schneider.

Tucker Cawley. Tucker was a writer's assistant. I read a spec script of Tucker's, thought it was great, and met with him. He told me hilarious stories of being an assistant to Tom Arnold during the fateful *Roseanne* years, complete with flying furniture. I had to hire him. He was also very funny, especially in his revulsion at Lew on Steve.

These were good decisions. Tucker, Lew, Steve, and Jeremy would stay with me for all nine years of the show.

Now, Ray wanted someone in The Room whom he knew, and who knew him very well, and would "represent" him while he was busy acting. So about two weeks into the process, a stand-up comedian named Tom Caltabiano was introduced to me, and we all resented his presence, for about five minutes. He, too, is very funny, and he very quickly became a double agent, fully understanding the challenges and hard work of writing scripts, and reporting back to Ray that he had nothing to worry about. Tom would also remain with us for nine years.

Why all the stand-ups? The basics and the structure of sitcom writing can be taught, being funny can't. Not all stand-ups can write stories and dialogue, but I happened to find brilliant ones who could. And when in doubt (write this down) people who make you pee on the floor laughing are good.

We started writing scripts. All outlines for stories went to the studios and then the network for approval. Iago disliked most of them and would tell Ray so. This made our job of trying to start up a series, which was already hard, harder. We never changed anything based on Iago's notes, but this was, at best, a pain in the ass. One of his notes was, "There are no real jokes here, this is all character stuff."

"Could you give me an example of the kind of joke you'd like to see instead?" I asked.

"Yeah. Someone could say, 'I like that hat.' And the other guy says, 'Really?' and the guy says, 'No.'"

I waited for more.

There wasn't any more. This friggin' guy was serious. And worse, dangerous. Because he had Ray's ear. He was a saboteur. What could I do? He was one of my bosses. Luckily I had plenty of other bosses, including Mr. Moonves, who had decided I was running this thing. And after making that decision, for the next nine years, Les Moonves never gave us a note. By the way, I never mind getting a constructive note. A good note can come from anywhere—the script supervisor, the cameraman, even a studio executive. They are, at the very least, people. And you want to make sure your show is coming across to people. That's who it's for. It could be that what you intended just isn't clear, and we learned that comedy isn't just comedy, it's clarity. Without that clarity, you're only funny to yourself. That said, what always ran in the back of my mind was Ed.'s "Do the show you want to do" and so, no matter what the note was or who it was from, my response was always the same—a very honest "We'll take a look at that."

Other than sticking to these principles, I really didn't know what the hell I was doing. I was a big shot with a show who would go home and pull his hair out wondering how the hell to actually run anything. What did I know? I had run a deli. Well, it turned out there were similarities. People come to you with problems, you make decisions. And they're all hungry. Who and how you are sets the tone. I didn't know exactly what kind of place I wanted work to be, but I thought, *Be nice.* Stupid sounding, yes, but I had worked at several places that weren't so nice. Sometimes the people in charge let the enormous pressures of success and failure get to them, and that affected how they were to everyone under them. Not so nice. One show I worked on, a memo got sent around:

"We've noticed that some of you are coming into the kitchen in the morning and pouring milk on your cereal. We do not provide breakfast for you. The cereals in the kitchen are snacks, the milk is for coffee only. Do not pour milk on your cereal." I remember thinking when I received this memo, *When I have my own show, we're going to have milk on our cereal.*

And we did.

We had the best food, the best craft service in town. This was crucial to me. Look, you're trying to create a family, on- and off-stage. If the food around is just sustenance, you grab it and move on. But if this cinnamon roll came in from Chicago, or the deli came in from New York, or once a year maybe stone crabs from Florida, you go to the craft service table and taste an amazing chocolate cake and turn to whoever is next to you and say, "Oh my God, this is good. Did you have this?" Right away, we're talking. And it's about something nice. It's a break that's nice in your day, no matter what the work is like. Ah, food. The other thing that could be nice is if the work is good, too, if it is actually something we could be proud of, which also didn't always happen on other shows I had been on, like *Baby Talk.* And so we worked very hard to make sure that was the case. We started with a few rules in The Writers' Room:

Could this happen? All the shows I valued took place on planet Earth—meaning, no matter what the situation, no matter how crazy, you *believed* that it could actually happen in real life. Everything had to be justified, and you couldn't sacrifice a character just for a joke. The moment something unbelievable happens in a show, the audience is taken out of the story, and if you do that enough, you lose its connection to the characters, and the show is weakened.

No topical jokes. Nothing dates a show sooner than a line about Monica Lewinsky. The show was for CBS, but in the back of my mind, it was for *Nick at Nite.*

No B stories. Most sitcoms, there's an A story (the main story) and a B story, to utilize the other cast members and to provide a respite from the A story. We figured, if a story is worth telling, it's worth telling for twenty minutes.

I had read that Carl Reiner, one of my idols, had run *The Dick Van Dyke Show* by asking his staff, "What happened at your house this week?" So I thought that this was the perfect methodology to use on *Raymond.*

The first episode after the pilot was "I Love You," and it was about how Ray never says those words to his wife, and she challenges him on it. I got to explore my own mishegoss and where that came from, and it felt good. The actors were great, and it seemed like this is where the show would live.

Steve Skrovan wrote a great script called "Standard Deviation," our third episode. It was about an IQ test that Robert administers to Ray and Debra, not to determine who's smarter but, as we found out at the end of the episode, to see how a husband and wife will react after *learning* who is smarter. There's a moment in there when Debra learns that Robert made a mistake on the test scores, and that Ray actually scored higher. Ray is a little smug about it, sitting next to her on the couch. Debra's eating ice cream at the time, and without a word, overturns her bowl and places it on Ray's lap. They sit there. Now, the audiences for these first few tapings have no prior knowledge of the show, don't know the characters except for what they've seen on the night they're there. The laugh for that moment, as Ray and Patty just sat there—Raymond knowing maybe he shouldn't have been smug, Debra's face saying, "You may be smarter but you now have a lap full of ice cream"—the laugh went on for more than thirty seconds. During that laugh, I realized we might be on to something bigger than just getting by. The audience not only found the characters funny, they knew the characters.

Not all the first-year episodes were great, and that was okay. I wanted every one to be perfect, but we were finding ourselves, and all shows need a little time to grow, to try things on and see if they fit. Networks and studios don't really have that time, however, and Iago knew it and took advantage of that. Eight episodes in, I wrote a script introducing Debra's parents entitled "In-Laws," and we were lucky enough to get Katherine Helmond and Robert Culp to play them.

We had a table read, then adjourned for notes with the network, the studio people, and Ray. Iago never attended table reads, but insisted on a closed-circuit feed to his office, and then would give his notes via speakerphone. "I don't like this episode and feel we shouldn't be doing it," he said.

"Why is that?" I asked, a reasonable question, but one that seemed to stump him.

"For one thing, it seems like we run out of story around page forty," he said.

I flipped through my script. "The script is forty pages long," I pointed out.

He couldn't get more specific. He just reiterated how bad he thought this script was.

When I got back to my office, I called him in private.

"What is going on?" I asked.

"You're really going to do a scene in a French restaurant?" he asked.

"Yes, what's wrong with that?"

"Hasn't that been done?"

"Well, hopefully not like this."

"But we've seen French restaurants before."

"Wait, you're talking about the set?"

"Yes. Why not make it a Japanese restaurant?"

"You don't like the French restaurant *set*? I don't get it. We've seen scenes in a bedroom, too. We still use that set," I said.

"I don't know what you're trying to do with this show," said Iago.

"What do you mean?"

"With the series. I mean, what kind of show are you trying to do?"

"I'm trying to do a well-made, traditional, classic type of sitcom."

And Iago said, "All words we should be avoiding."

I took a second. "And what words should we be running toward?"

And Iago said, "Hip and edgy."

I said, "Well, you've got the right guy, because I am Mr. Hip and Edgy."

I couldn't figure it out. If this was his attempt at a coup, it seemed insane. Maybe a sushi bar set was the proper edginess that could have patched our relationship, but things got worse that week, as Iago chose this episode to demonstrate to everyone and especially Ray why I should be replaced. I started getting calls from other executives that Ray wasn't happy, and that I would have to talk to him. What the hell? I thought my relationship with Ray was fine—we talked as much as we needed to, seeing as how Ray is uncomfortable having a one-on-one talk with anyone. And besides, the show seemed to be going well. We had some episodes that were better than others, but certainly none you'd consider bad yet. One executive tried to make sense of it for me by sitting me down and saying, "The show is going like this"—as he made a circular motion with his fingers—"when it should be going like this." And he reversed the circular motion of his fingers.

This executive would later claim to have "saved the show."

When I called Ray, I asked what was wrong, and he couldn't really be specific, either, but he did mention Iago a couple of times. I tried to assure Ray that we were really fine, and that if he ever had any specific doubts or problems he should come to me. But what could I do if he didn't inherently trust me?

I was getting nervous. And on shoot night, I knew we had to have a good show to prove to everyone that . . . we had a good show. And that I was good. I opened the door to the makeup room, where the actors gather before we shoot to run lines, to give a pep talk. I must have been a nervous wreck because I said, "Listen, everybody's got to step up this episode. And everybody's got to be really great tonight, all right? So just get out there and really give it everything you've got." This didn't come from an inspiring football coach place. It came from a wrinkly kid who's nervous about losing his job. The actors just stared at me and said, "Uh, yeah, thanks a lot." Like we're not trying? I regretted doing that, but I had nowhere to go with that energy. I needed them. I didn't have anybody else. I needed them to come through. And of course, they did, as usual. Is it our best episode? It was good enough for the moment. And at the very least, it was a good introduction to Katherine Helmond and Robert Culp, who've endured through the years. It was good enough that Iago couldn't bother me for a while.

Let's talk about Ray. Ray is a naturally gifted actor, with the ability to project his true nature (a warm, affable, "regular" guy) to the audience, and to do so with great humor. What's most amazing about his performance on our show is that before the show, he had never really acted and was understandably nervous. So nervous that he did not want to do anything on the show that he, Ray Romano, did not actually do in real life. He would not drink coffee in a scene because he didn't drink coffee in real life. I suggested that, this being television, we could put anything he wanted in the cup. Ray still wouldn't do it. "They won't believe it," he said. As crazy as this sounds, this is an actor who cares, above all else, about being believable—perhaps the number-one job of any actor. So it was a process of taking chances, of exploring things outside himself that Ray started to learn how to do during these first few months. And every time he took a chance, he succeeded. It helped that next to him was Patty Heaton, a great actress, and that they were surrounded by a superb supporting cast. It helped that Ray worked with Richard Marion, an acting coach, every week at home on the material, and I helped him with becoming comfortable enough to try stuff. A couple of episodes later, we really needed him to drink the coffee. He said, "All right, at some point I have to start acting, I guess."

The real challenge came on our first Christmas episode, number twelve, "The Ball." The climactic scene called for Ray to discover the real reason his father forged Mickey Mantle's signature on a baseball for him when he was a kid. It turned out that Frank had waited outside the stadium for days, and Mantle wouldn't see him, and Frank didn't want to disappoint Raymond, so he practiced Mantle's signature and gave his son the ball. When Ray finally hears his father explain it, all these years later, he's so touched by it that the script calls for him to cross to his dad, who is sitting at the kitchen table, and give him a kiss on the head.

"No way would that ever happen," said Ray, stopping rehearsal.

I didn't understand. But Ray insisted that he would never, ever kiss his father.

"Okay, but could you see that a son *could* kiss his dad?" I asked.

"It would never happen," he said and he started getting upset in front of everyone at rehearsal.

I took him aside and told him he certainly didn't have to do the kiss, and that I wouldn't ask him to anymore. Forget about it for now. "But," I said to Ray, "come shoot night, if you get to that moment, and you *feel* it . . . do it."

A few nights later, we're shooting the show, and here comes that scene. It's going well, and we get to that moment, and Ray crosses to his father . . . and kisses him on the head. What a guy. I'm telling you, yes, it's just a sitcom, but there wasn't a dry eye in the house. And it was because it came from a guy you would never expect to do something like that.

The rest of that season had lots of wonderful moments like that—moments of discovery for all of us, and the realization that maybe we were on to something special.

We needed a date for Robert, and so we thought of Monica to

play Amy, a friend of Debra's who first appeared in episode fourteen. She seemed to work out, and that became one of the great pleasures in my life—having Monica with me there, and having other people getting what I got about her. The only problem was that everyone on staff started to love her more than they loved me. Just like my family.

Tucker Cawley wrote a script, episode seventeen, "The Game," in which the cable TV goes out one night, and the Barones are forced to talk to one another. They play a game, a real board game called Scruples and we find out just who's got 'em and who doesn't. This was the first episode we did that took place entirely in one room, in real time, and we found that the characters were strong enough to sustain such immobility. We were happy doing theater, little plays, and we knew the focus would always be on content—writing and acting, not hairstyles or set changes, or nipples poking through T-shirts. (Some sets around town are kept extra cold for just such reasons.)

We were still getting notes from the execs: "Ray should help out more around the house or women won't like him." To which I could only ask, "Then why did they marry him?"

"The brother scares me. I'd have less of the brother."

"They shouldn't argue so much. It's not likable."

"Likable" is a terrible television word. Let me ask you something: Who in your family is "likable"?

But Doris Roberts was a little afraid of the arguing, too. She was a veteran of stage and screen, and where she was coming from, likable was important to her. She didn't want to bicker with her on-screen husband. In fact, Doris told me that she had gotten great advice when starting in television: "The victim wins the Emmy."

Oy. Obviously, this was not what I had in mind for Marie. But Doris had already won an Emmy for her performance in *St. Elsewhere* as a homeless woman who loses her homeless man. Great for *St. Elsewhere,* but the victim is far from a comedic choice. We needed Marie to be strong, to stand up to Frank, to intrude, butt in, be jealous of her daughter-in-law, favor one son over the other, to be anything *but* a victim. In fact, how could I tell Doris she was supposed to be the villain of the show?

What could I tell her to justify such behavior?

I told her, "Everything you do comes from love."

That was all Doris needed as an actress, and she was undeniably, absolutely brilliant in the role of Marie, going on to win four Emmys, and thank God, never once as the victim.

As these weeks went by, I was learning and getting used to running things. A good deal of becoming a showrunner is trial by fire—you think you might know how to drive a car but you don't until you're actually behind the wheel (and your father is yelling, "What the hell are you doing, you'll kill us all!").

I learned as a showrunner how to talk to the actors—not just how to communicate what we were thinking in The Writers' Room when we wrote a particular script, but motivation, timing, inflection, even facial expression, all, I hoped, to help with getting the most out of each moment. And I learned that on show night when the studio audience was there, if the actors flubbed a line or there was a sound or camera glitch, how to yell "Hold!" This was to pause the action, because the next joke or story point might depend on the setup that we just missed, and if that clarity was gone, the whole scene could be derailed. So we'd stop and go back to get a clean run at it.

We were looking for the feeling of a live theatrical event, a play captured on film, and yet our out-of-town tryout was take one. There's only one take one—just one time the material lands on virgin ears and just one chance to get that first-time-you-heard-it-laugh. So if something's not going how it should, anywhere in your life, don't continue and risk making it worse, always yell "Hold!"

The other most important thing I learned was the magic of editing. We actually referred to this in the episode "Robert's Wedding" during Ray's speech at the reception: We all have internal editing capabilities that make some of life's unbearable moments (like Marie's objecting to the wedding during the ceremony) a bit more bearable through our selective memories. Well, in television we actually have *machines* that can literally edit out lousy jokes, bad passages of writing, too much acting, camera accidents, coughs, someone in the audience saying a line along with the actors (my father did that once). We can create a dramatic pause if there wasn't one, comic timing where necessary, whole performances—whole episodes—can be made or lost in the editing room, and so no matter how the show is going that week, you still have one last shot to save your career.

In January of that first season, Les Moonves called me into his office to tell me that starting in March, our show would be moving to Monday night, after *Cosby,* for a trial run.

Mr. Moonves said, "We like you, the critics like you, but if you don't perform on Mondays, we can't help you anymore."

I hadn't been nervous in a while, and now here was another nice shot of oy. We had been somewhat protected in our Friday night slot following *Dave's World.* Nobody expected big numbers there, and they didn't get them. But now, on CBS's Monday night, between *Cosby* and *Murphy Brown,* people were expected to watch. It was wonderful, as in "You made the play-offs!" But, like in the play-offs, you could be sent home at anytime. The first Monday at eight-thirty, our ratings doubled.

I was happy, right? No. I was more nervous than ever. Because we had been sampled. People watched. And now . . . we had nowhere to go but down.

I told you I was Jewish, yes?

Ray understood. He was pessimistic, too, and could always find the bad in any given situation—that's one of the things I like most about him. The numbers came in for the following week . . . and they went up. Up? This stumped both Ray and me. "A bad football game on the other channel," Ray postulated. But I was actually encouraged. Variety reported, "With those numbers, it looks like *Raymond* has found a permanent spot on Monday nights." I clipped that little mention and kept it in my wallet. I stopped being nervous.

After filming twenty-two episodes, we finished the first season and went to New York for a meeting with the two studios to talk about how it went and how we'd proceed for next season. I entered the conference room, where Ray and all the key people were gathered, and noticed that everyone had binders, official binders with one of the studio's logos on the cover. "What's that?" I asked. It was thirty pages of criticism. Episode by episode. Thirty pages of what was wrong with *Raymond,* written by Iago. It had been distributed to everyone but me the night before.

I'm not a violent man. I'm so not violent, I rarely even use the word in a sentence. When I get angry, people usually laugh. But I approached Iago. I quietly demanded an explanation.

"You didn't get this?" asked Iago innocently. "I had it sent to where you were staying. Hmp. Everyone else got it."

Steam was coming out of my ears because I had put up with enough. I couldn't believe it. I was shaking. How could someone do this? I was about to, if not hit him, certainly make a scene that involved bad language, when one of the other studio people took me aside and whispered, "Don't worry about this." I said, "Did you read it?" He answered, "I don't have to. Nobody read it. Nobody cared. They saw through him. It's okay, believe me. We're a hit."

It still bothered me, but the fact that Iago's last desperate swipe at my job was ignored made me feel a little better.

From then on we didn't have to broadcast our table reads to Iago's office anymore. We didn't get notes from him anymore. He mysteriously stopped caring about the quality of the show. He worked on new ways to get out of his studio job, but Iago never bothered me again.

We had a great, festive wrap party. David Letterman filmed a special "Top Ten" list for us, we showed our first gag reel, and really laughed together. We were all proud of what we'd done and happy that we were some of the lucky few who get to keep doing it.

During all the dancing and eating and drinking, Ray came over and handed me a note in an envelope. I later found a quiet corner of the room and opened it. The note said, "I never thought I'd thank anyone for making me kiss Peter Boyle."

7

Nothing But Sex

Sorry, I'm just thinking the chapter titles should get better as the book goes along. I ran into the great Garry Marshall (*The Odd Couple, Happy Days, Laverne and Shirley, Pretty Woman*) at a CBS end-of-year party, and he asked me what season we were going into. I told him the second. He looked wistful and said, "Ahh. I love the second season." He had been there many times. He knew that having done the hardest part—creating a world and trying to establish characters who lived there over the first twenty-two episodes—the second season was always easier.

I loved having finished the first season alive, and that people were happy, and that we could now go on vacation . . . yes, and maybe have some sex, but first . . . I had to fire a guy. Now, I had been fired before, myself, at least three times—the museum, the movie company, that unhappy New York show—and I never really enjoyed the experience. But this was a whole new set of awful. This was ruining someone else's life. But this fellow wasn't pulling his weight in The Room, he wasn't writing good drafts of scripts, and he was the most negative guy in the world, especially given that he had a pretty good job with great food. At one point, after delivering a very weak script, we gave him notes and gave him another shot at it. He said, "Can someone else do this next draft? I'm really burned out on this thing." He had only done one draft. Maybe he wanted us to clip his toenails for him, too. And by the way, if you saw him, not a terrible idea.

During a table reading of one of Lew's scripts, this guy, let's call him Rasputin, sat in plain sight with his arms folded and didn't crack a smile once. When we got back to the room, Lew was furious. "I take umbrage!" he said very seriously to Rasputin, to which Rasputin chuckled, both at the idea that he had made Lew so angry by not laughing, and at the use of the word "umbrage" among people in this century. But that made Lew, a generally jovial man (even when not having intercourse with the thermostat), madder. "I take *severe* umbrage!" He was standing over Rasputin. Lew may have chosen his words poorly for a room full of comedians, but his anger was righteous. We are a team, we work on the scripts together, no matter whose name is on it, and we support one another. There's no written rule that you have to laugh at everything, but when you sit at a table reading or rehearsal, no matter what you think, you can at least muster up a pleasant demeanor for your brother or sister writer, not to mention actor. To not do so is bad sportsmanship and bad for business.

But this wasn't why I had to fire Rasputin. I had to fire him because every word, sound, and smell that came out of him, on and off paper, broadcast that he didn't want the job. So after we wrapped the first season, I called him to come into the office. My stomach hurt. I told him it just wasn't working out and that I had to make a change for next season. He laughed and thought I was kidding. I'm not a very tough-looking character. When I tell my kids to brush their teeth, they make fart noises at me. But I now had to let this man know I was, sadly, serious. He got it. Here's what he said: "I can't believe you're doing this to me."

"I'm sorry, Rasputin."

"My kids are sick, man."

His kids weren't sick. But he actually thought he might try that gambit, considering my reputation as Mister Softee. Over the whole nine years, I had to fire about 5 percent of our writing workforce, men and women, always, ultimately, for the same reason. No matter how crazy or difficult they were to get along with (and that's no small consideration when you're locked in a room with others all day), they were tolerated as long as the work was sound. But if the work wasn't great *and* they were nuts . . . what could you do? I hated confrontation so much that in one case I let someone slide for five years. The last straw was when I found out that person was sneaking into my office and opening the mail on my desk. Why are so many people nutsy in show business? I guess sometimes the thing that makes you good is the same thing that makes you crazy. Usually, in time, crazy wins. "So why do you hire these people in the first place?" I hear you asking. Because it always starts well.

One title I was considering for this book was *Everyone's Nice in the Meeting.* That's true. I find that it's only when you really get to know people that they make you fear them. Most writers I'd hire had good credits, and then I'd find out that maybe they didn't write that *Seinfeld* script I read and hired them off of by themselves, but they're now on board the show and writing under false pretenses. This actually happens quite often, and can be added to the list of reasons why television is mostly smelly.

In April 1997, after wrapping our first season, I had an idea to make life less fun for some more people. The writers couldn't just go on vacation—CBS had ordered twenty-four episodes for our upcoming second season, and I knew we had to get a jump on these stories. So I decided that nobody was leaving (even though we were exhausted) until we each had a story that went to the outline stage, and that the outlines were strong. This took two more weeks. And with the six-week hiatus that we had left before preproduction officially started, we were each going to write a draft over "vacation."

Where the hell did this come from? I certainly was never like this in school. I was the kid who let his homework wait till Sunday night and then probably didn't do it. But now, was I . . . growing up?

I did feel I had a real responsibility, and other people were depending on me, so I took the leadership part of the job as seriously as the jokes and food part. It's kind of a left-brain, right-brain thing where you *want* to be the Room monkey (I always was on the other shows I worked on), but as the showrunner you also have to have that other part—the organizational, the managerial, the financially responsible guy, all of which I am naturally not. For example, when I hear more than three numbers in a row, I fall into a coma.

I had worked on shows where not only were these two months of April and May considered hiatus, but the following two months of preproduction were also treated as vacation, because the pressure was not immediate—it's summer, there's no show next week, so we can hang out, work a little, go to lunch, go to the movies, shoot craps, all of which I thought we could have time for, too . . . if we just did some of this work now.

So this was the start of the system. And it was hard that first season going into the second, because at this point we weren't ahead, we had just made it to the finish line with our tongues hanging out, and now: more work. So I was King Dick for a week or two. The writers were kvetching while we were pitching out stories. "Why do we have to?"

"I'm telling you, our lives will be better." I knew it would work because I'd been on shows where we were so behind all the time. The schedule is just this boulder coming down on your head every week.

The writers were great about it, and we did it, and when we came back to work June 1 of that second season we had ten first drafts.

Instead of taking that preproduction of two months to come up with stories and write them quickly, we already had a good chunk of the season finished. And while we were tabling (improving) those drafts, people were coming up with their next stories already. From then on, by the time we started production every August, we knew what every story for the season would be, and we had half of the scripts completely polished, finished. We now had time for hanging out, movies, dice games, long lunches, and going home early. The going home early part was actually essential to *Raymond.* Home was where the material was coming from. We'd come to work at ten A.M. and, in nine years, we were always home for dinner by seven o'clock, and usually by six. This was important. You can't write about real life unless you have one.

And I was having one. Right before we started production on season two, our second child, Lily, was born: a beautiful blonde with a hilarious personality who would go on to make life hell for her brother. The day after Lily arrived, all the writers and their families came to visit us in the hospital. We sat around Monica's bed, eating deli sandwiches, drinking, and corrupting the baby with salty language. I look back fondly on this time as one of my all-time favorite births.

It was also around this time that my agent and I learned that The Powers That Be would not be giving me even a modest raise going into season two, but were only going to stick to the 5 percent bump that was in the original contract. Now, after one year, the show was their number-one sitcom, and you'd think a bit of renegotiation might be in order, especially for the lowest-paid showrunner in town. But The Powers That Be didn't have to give me any more, and you should know that if they don't have to, they don't. As luck would have it, that same week, some nice people at Disney Studios called and offered me a development deal. It was for a lot of money. It was for millions and millions of dollars. They just wanted me to fly to New York to meet with the president of their television division. So I took a sick day during preproduction and snuck off to

New York for the meeting. But before the meeting, since I was in New York, I thought I'd grab lunch with my brother at one of my favorite restaurants, Jean Georges. Maybe I'll get a coupon in the mail. My brother and I were having a great time, a great lunch, when who should walk into the restaurant but a big important executive for whom I happened to be working. This executive knew that I should be in Los Angeles working on *Raymond,* and he had that look in his eye of "what are you doing here?" But he was with some TV station owners who recognized me and so he could only happily introduce me, and we all said hello with big smiles and continued on to enjoy our lunches.

I then went to the meeting with Mr. Disney Television, and he told me that they really wanted to make the deal with me. I'd just have to leave *Raymond* and come work for them. Well, I knew I couldn't do that. The show was already special to me, and I said no, thank you, and flew home. But I used Disney's offer as a bargaining chip in an effort to get a bit more money at *Raymond.* Do you know what happened? I didn't get it. The Powers That Be said, "No. We'll understand if you have to go." Well . . . there's an awkward moment. Why were they treating me this way? Simple: I was a stupid businessman. I wore my heart on my sleeve about this show, and you could say I allowed myself to be taken advantage of.

The next day the phone rang and the Disney people said I wouldn't have to leave *Raymond* now, I could wait and come to Disney at the end of the season . . . same money. Done. I took the deal. I would've been an idiot to turn this down—remember, *Raymond* wasn't worth any money yet, I just loved it. The next day, a man came to my front door holding a check for a million dollars—an advance from Disney. I had never seen a million dollars, and to be honest, it scared the hell out of me. I told him to give it to the lady of the house, and he walked into our living room and gave the check to Monica, who was nursing Lily at the time and almost dropped her.

So we began the second season with a sense of security, and all was pleasant. We did an episode called "Brother" in which we explored Robert's character, trying to flesh him out and make him more than just a giant punch line. Brad rose to the occasion and showed great sensitivity, especially when he learned that Raymond had only spent an evening with him because their mother forced him to. If the first season of a show is about introducing the characters, we thought the second season should be about deepening them, exploring what other sides there were, and understanding what made them tick. For example, I wrote one called "Mozart" based on my own mother's love of classical music, and Ray's mother's actual occupation as a Juilliard-trained piano teacher. My mother always wanted to impart the importance of music to us, and so this episode was a way of showing her I got it, and appreciated it, and appreciated her, in between all the fruit jokes at her expense. We wrote one called "Anniversary," which was based on the real-life, onetime separation of Ray's parents. In our episode we thought it would be interesting for Ray to find out on the day that he's throwing them a surprise fortieth-anniversary party that his parents had actually been separated for a while when he was a kid.

We thought of a way to illustrate the story in flashback, by having Ray and Patty play the younger versions of Marie and Frank. This would be more fun than having outside actors cast as the Barone parents, and cheaper, too. (See, left brain–right brain.) We had Ray and Patty pantomime silently while Peter and Doris narrated, and when Ray or Patty spoke in this flashback, they would lip-synch to Peter's and Doris's voices. We thought this was a great device and fun. Well, at the table reading of this episode, you couldn't obviously see what Ray and Patty would look like when they were made up to be Marie and Frank. The lip-synching hadn't been worked out yet, and so the laughs were understandably smaller than we knew they'd be on show night. I say "understandably" because I assumed most people would understand that. And I hoped that people would get the bigger joke underneath all this, which was: We become our parents. A couple of executives approached. "We don't think this episode works."

"Okay," I said. "Why's that?"

"We don't know. It might be that flashback thing."

"Okay," I said. "We'll take a look at that."

And we did. And, as is our prerogative, we left it as is. The next day, the two execs came up to me again. "You didn't change it. We're still really worried about this episode," they said and they did indeed look very worried. I told them not to worry about it: We were pretty sure it would be fine. The part they were worried about was physical, and we'd wait to judge it after seeing everyone in hair and makeup.

After run-through that day, Ray came up to me. He told me that two executives had cornered him and told him how worried they were about this week's episode, and that they weren't getting anywhere with me, so they went to him.

The next morning, I called a meeting. This was the first time I had called a meeting involving network or studio people. When we all sat down, I very calmly (on the outside) told them that I either was the showrunner or I wasn't. But if I was, I had to be allowed to run the show. The next time someone went to Ray or another actor or anyone else on the show behind my back, I wouldn't be coming in the next day. And I left the meeting. I sound tough, huh? I was shaking. But the next day, both of the execs came to me, apologizing. One extended an envelope to me. "Is this a coupon?" I asked. "It's an explanation," said the exec. I politely refused to take the envelope.

I wasn't trying to be rude, but I didn't care what the explanation was. It didn't matter. This just could never happen again. "But I need you to understand the reason why I did it," the exec pleaded. I didn't care why this person did it. And not only did I not care about the reason, I wouldn't have believed the reason. There are politics in every office, and it's no different in the so-called creative arts. In fact it might be worse because of the creative ways creative people try to advance in the business. It's the part of the business that makes you sick.

I shouldn't say *the* part. It's only one of the parts, and only a few of them can be discussed here—not just because of etiquette, but because of space. There were some thrilling high points in that second season: "The Letter" was one of my favorites. We took a perfectly good script written by Kathy Stumpe and really got something going in The Room. Debra has a Tupperware party in the first act that Marie ruins—that was pretty standard sitcom fare. But in the second act, and this is where we found the series' true strength, Debra writes Marie a letter, outlining exactly what's wrong with their relationship. My mother enjoys writing a "scathing letter" now and then, and my wife has been a recipient as well as a writer of such missives. It's a little difficult to live with such people sometimes, and by "such people" I mean all wives and mothers. So this situation seemed to not only bring to a head the central conflicts in our show, but some fundamental differences between men and women. Women fight, then make up with hugging and crying—it's cathartic to them, and somehow, for some primal reason, necessary. Men watch this and scratch their heads. We had Frank say, "That's a fight? I'm glad we didn't order that on pay-per-view."

The actors, every one of them, were brilliant in that episode, everyone firing on all cylinders, and when you see that episode, you're seeing one, uninterrupted take of that long scene—where Frank gleefully reads aloud Debra's letter to Marie, Marie glowers, Ray tries to deny the letter's existence, Robert looks for cover, and Debra enters the scene thinking perhaps she shouldn't have sent it. It was like a great evening in the theater, and the next day, as we gathered to read the following week's script, I had to say to our cast, staff, and crew family, "Years from now, if people ask me, 'Did you realize how special it was at the time?' I will say yes."

As the season progressed, we had "Marie's Meatballs" by Susan

Van Allen (where Marie sabotages Debra's attempts to cook and in effect "gaslights" her), "T-Ball" by the now de-umbraged Lew Schneider (where Ray and Debra clash over finding a list-approved snack for the kids' softball team), "The Ride Along" by Jeremy Stevens (where we get some insight as to just how Marie feels about Robert's being a policeman), "Traffic School" by Kathy Stumpe (where Robert practices his official traffic school spiel on the family with the aid of Traffic Cop Timmy, a ventriloquist's dummy), and "Good Girls."

"Good Girls," by Tucker Cawley, was exceptional in that the revelations of the second act (where we find out just who was a "good girl" before marriage and who wasn't) were received like a succession of fireworks by the studio audience. The final revelation, that Robert was, in fact, illegitimately conceived, topped everything, and was one of the more satisfying tapings we ever had. Again, the actors were superb, and again, like theater, they played right through that second act in the first take without stopping, and that's what you see on film. What you can't see is me, behind the monitors, filling up with tears at how well it was going, that this kind of work and reception was beyond any hopes I had ever had. What a joy.

And so, at the end of that second season, when it was time to go to Disney, I asked them if I could postpone, if I could have one more season on *Raymond.* They said yes. I was happy. I didn't have a contract beyond season two on *Raymond,* and I didn't care. The ratings were up, we were now a top-ten show. Surely the people I was doing the show for would take care of me.

Well, as famed producer, author, and then book-on-tape autobiographer Robert Evans says, "You bet your ass they . . . didn't." I came back to work on the show in season three without a contract. I was an idiot, but a happy one. We did our stay-ahead system of writing a script each over hiatus, and when we returned to preproduction that year, there was a new surprise: Now that it looked as if we were a hit and might very well make it into syndication, the studios that produced the show decided they didn't want to put any more money into it.

Why? When we started, the studios wanted a very low risk. So they didn't put a lot of money up to begin with—they were betting on the show to lose. When you make that bet in Vegas, your return will not be that great. So now, they only wanted to get money back. CBS said, "Well, that's ridiculous. We're not going to deficit [pay for] the entire show." And the studios said, "Well, you get most of the back end from syndication, so you deficit it." And CBS said no. So during preproduction, I got a list of the things the studio said *Raymond* was now going to have to do without.

Are you ready?

The audience.

Yes, no studio audience.

No swing sets, meaning no sets other than the permanent set, just Ray and Debra's living room and kitchen. Not even Marie and Frank's house? No, that's not a permanent set. That's a swing set because we don't use it every single show. Ray's living room and kitchen, we use every show. If you were to come and sit in the audience, that is the set right in front of you. The other sets are along the side. You could see them from the audience, but usually you'd watch a TV monitor right above you to see what the cameras were getting. If we built Nemo's Restaurant, or Robert's apartment, those were swing sets.

And we couldn't have any of those.

No guest cast.

No craft service. Now they're hitting me where I live. No food. Bring your own.

So why was I getting this list? This was obviously insane. What the studio people wanted was to force me into calling CBS and saying, "I can't do the show this year." I would be forced into saying to Les Moonves, "You have to help me. You have to step up." The studios were using me to get CBS to pay for everything because they didn't want to pay for it. CBS knows no one can do a show without these essentials, so they were going to have to pay for them.

Did the studios have to do this to me? No, they could have sent that letter to Les directly, but they sent it to me, making me do their work for them. And rather than saying to me, like a person, "We need you to do this," they just sent me this thing, like I'm a pawn. And that's how I felt.

So I was furious and annoyed at everybody. It was hard enough to make a freakin' show; I didn't need these politics. I didn't need to be in the middle of this petty crap and I didn't need to really worry that everyone's life on the show was going to be miserable. Of course I wound up having to go to Les Moonves, and of course he said, "Those sons of bitches. Don't worry. I'll take care of it." And of course he did, and we started the third season.

But I wanted to make sure this wouldn't happen to me again. We had the first table reading, and the studio representatives came over to me and said, "Oh, we're so glad it all worked out." I said, "Yeah, it all worked out. I really resent the position you put me in, and I'm really angry about it. So from now on, please don't talk to me. Your notes are welcome. You can give them to my writers' assistant, but don't give them to me. I don't want to hear from you guys directly anymore. I'm not telling you you can't do your jobs. I'm not telling you you can't be here, but I don't like the way you've communicated with me lately, and I'm not interested anymore. So please give your notes to the writers' assistant." They were stunned. They flipped out. They started leaving me messages begging me to reconsider. They started sending gifts to my house like cookies and Krispy Kreme donuts.

This is a good snapshot of phony-baloney Hollywood. These people could do their jobs by giving their notes to a writers' assistant, but they didn't want to. Their sense of their own personal status had to do with interacting with the showrunner directly.

A week later I was talking to them again. I don't like that feeling, you know? That people are upset, and there's tension. It's a bad feeling, and I had made my point. What I really wanted was everyone—crew, staff, network and studio people, any visitors at all—to come to our set on Stage 5 at Warner Brothers and have a great time and be happy. I thought it would reflect in the work, and besides, I don't want to have an enemy. Who wants an enemy? I operate under the assumption that most people are very nice, and that you should be nice and that's how the world works. And then I'm always stunned when . . . it's not.

At the end of the day, you know the best way to reconcile your feelings with people who've done you wrong? Just keep this in mind: They have to be them. That's their punishment. Iago goes to bed at night and when he wakes up in the morning, still has to be Iago. I get to be me. You want to trade? No. Would you like to trade with the asshole who hurt you? I would not. I would like to trade with Mr. Justin Timberlake.

So the third season begins, and here's a little more news: Our time slot is moving to nine P.M. Monday. I hadn't been nervous about the show's life for a while and here was a golden Jewish opportunity to worry some more. At nine P.M. Monday, we would now be opposite the two biggest shows in the country: *Monday Night Football* and the show of the moment, *Ally McBeal.* I was positive our nice little ride was about to end. Within three months we were beating both of them. This was amazing to me, and especially gratifying to beat *Football,* because I had been picked on by jocks my whole adolescence, boys who didn't understand that the drama club was a valid form of self-expression, too.

The series was taking off. I was in The Writers' Room with the guys, and the phone rang. "Phil, Mary Tyler Moore is on line one." And I picked up the phone and there was Mary Tyler Moore calling just because she liked the show. "Phil, it's Mary!" she said, sounding a lot like Mary Tyler Moore. I told Mary I was plotzing that she would call me and, because she had a Jewish husband, I didn't have to explain "plotzing."

Norman Lear called, saying, "I hear we're fans of each other. We should have lunch." Whose life was this? Mr. Lear said, "And if you don't mind, I have a friend who'd like to join us." So I went to lunch at Pinot on Ventura Boulevard with Norman Lear and his friend Carl Reiner. I had a wonderful time with them, these fantastically talented, funny, warm guys, who felt like family right away. I came home from lunch that day and dropped dead. Because of the show, I've gotten to meet, and even become friendly with, my absolute idols. They say you should never meet your idols, but I've only loved it every time. I can't speak for how it was for the idols.

And then the work itself was so rewarding. Steve Skrovan had an idea before we started shooting season one that involved Frank's handing out brightly colored condoms, which he mistakenly thinks are candies, to Halloween trick-or-treaters. CBS advised us not to do this the first season, especially because we were on Friday at eight-thirty, and we were fine with that. But now, season three, nine P.M. . . . we said to CBS, "Remember that story idea . . . ?" They said, "Do whatever you want." We had always wanted to do an adult show about families, and "Halloween Candy" was a pretty good example of the tone we tried to set in the series. In nine years we never got one Standards and Practices note from the network. (It seems that department has disappeared from the land.) But we still, always, took very seriously the responsibility of being on television. We knew that even at nine P.M. children might be watching, so we governed ourselves.

For instance, in that episode we never used the words "condoms" or even "contraception." We said "things" and "stuff." Grown-ups knew what we meant. It's funnier to be oblique sometimes, and we might have saved kids' questions to their parents for another day.

I had some other favorites that year: Susan Van Allen and Ellen Sandler wrote "No Fat," which costarred a particularly gelatinous tofu turkey. Jeremy Stevens wrote one of our most popular episodes, "Robert's Date," where Robert goes out dancing with his black partner and, upon returning, starts to affect certain urban mannerisms, like saying to Ray, "You gotta get out more, my brutha." And then there was "The Toaster."

The previous holiday season I had given everyone a toaster with the name of our show engraved on the side as my cast and crew gift for that year—a nice little present, I thought. And so I sent one to my parents, knowing they would enjoy it because they were proud of the show and reportedly liked me. Two weeks went by, and I didn't hear from them. So I thought I should call them in New York and make sure they had received it. My father answered the phone. I asked him if they got my Hanukkah present.

"What?" said my father in a trademarked Yiddish accent.

"The present I sent you," I said. "Did you get it?"

"Oh. Yes, yes, thank you, very nice."

And that was it.

"Did you see what it was?"

"What. It was a toaster. What."

Now I knew what had happened. He wasn't excited because they hadn't opened the box and seen the engraving.

"It's not just a toaster, Dad, you have to open the box—go, go get the box, open it up, go ahead."

There was a long pause, and finally my father said, "I don't have it with me right now."

My eyes narrowed. I asked slowly, "What did you do?"

Another long pause and he said, "Your mother wanted a coffee-maker."

Yes. They took my toaster to Bloomingdale's, *lied to them,* and traded my gift for a coffeemaker.

I was in my office at work when I made this call, and soon several of my colleagues were rushing into my office because they heard me screaming.

"You are the show! Do you realize you are the show?! You are the reason we have a show!"

And my father said, "You're welcome."

I was livid. What the hell kind of parents were these? I spent a lot of time thinking about the perfect present, and every time I sent them anything, it was no good. Of course, my fellow writers told me that this was an episode, and that I had to write it, and I refused for a very good reason. This wasn't funny. Yes, I ultimately calmed down and wrote the episode. And as it turned out with many of our personal stories, the writing was actually therapeutic.

Our joke in The Room was that someone probably went to Bloomingdale's, got that returned toaster, brought it home, opened it up, and then brought it back to Bloomingdale's and said, "I'd like the *Frasier* toaster."

There was one more episode that season, which, if you were to ask Ray or me to pick a favorite of the series, this might be it. It was our traditional end-of-the-season flashback episode, and this one was called "How They Met." Raymond and I wrote it together, and it recounted the saga of when Ray and Debra met. Again, we incorporated some real life in there—Ray really had worked for a futon delivery service, "Claude's Futons," but the heart and soul of the show revolved around the second act, which depicted Ray and Debra's first date in Debra's little apartment. In performance, Ray and Patty were so funny and so sweet and touching, you could hear the audience members' hearts melting. Not only is it the first time they kiss, it's the first time Ray tastes Debra's lemon chicken. "You really like it?" asks Debra. "You kidding?" says Raymond. "I could eat this the rest of my life."

To me, this is why people get married. You have no idea what's coming, you're just in love. And stupid. Ray doesn't yet realize that the chicken is the only thing she can make.

When we dissolve back to the present day in that episode, fifteen years later, there's a wistful look on Ray's and Debra's faces, and then Debra slaps a piece of lemon chicken onto Raymond's plate. This is marriage.

The episodes we were doing were so creatively satisfying, so much fun to do, and the response was so overwhelming from people that I knew I had a big problem: Disney. I would definitely have to leave *Raymond* at the end of this season—I couldn't put them off anymore, I had taken their money. Besides, I was still working without a contract on *Raymond,* which was financially dumb. And so I wrestled with this, and then I did the only thing I could possibly do—I gave Disney back the money.

On to season four.

8

This Is How We Do It

Sorry, still not about sex. We're going to talk about the process, at the end of which, if done correctly, you will not yell, "True, but dull!"

But first, what about my deal? I still didn't have one, but sometimes things work out. I had given Disney their money back, which they graciously accepted, but six months later a giant conglomerate, Viacom (which owns CBS), bought Paramount Studios, and now I could make a development deal with Paramount while remaining on *Raymond* because both companies were now owned by the same wonderful giant conglomerate. And that's what I did. I now had nothing to complain about, but I was sure I'd find something.

You know what I hate? Having to explain a joke. This chapter isn't that, I promise, but it may come close, because it's about The Writers' Room. You see, The Room is mainly an inside joke. What happens in there is probably only funny to the people in there, because the people in there are very close—it's as if someone comes up to you and says, "If you come to my office for the day, you'll be able to make a sitcom out of it!" My answer to this is usually: I find that highly unlikely. Yes, it's funny to you, nice friend of my parents, because you're there every day, you know all the characters, the dynamics, the situations, and yet the hilarity at the south end of the third floor at the accounting firm of Liebman and Strunk may not translate to everyone. "Yes, but my office really *is* a sitcom!" they insist. And then I say, "I can't go to weddings anymore."

Let's get to know our situation in The Writers' Room a little better. We're in a room with a big rectangular table in it that seats about ten. We're all in those nice Aeron chairs with the adjustable lumbar support because we're very old. I'm not at the head of the table, I'm on the side near a smaller table on which sits the Mighty Wurlitzer, the computer, and I can see what our writers' assistant is typing into it at any given moment. And I'm reading aloud to the rest of the congregation, who are usually playing with Silly Putty, reading *Variety,* sleeping, or humping the thermostat.

We don't start out that way . . . we usually come in about ten A.M., get our coffee, bagels, and cereal (with milk!), and sit and talk. And talk and talk and talk, usually in an effort to avoid working. What we're talking about is everything you talk about when you're supposed to be working: home, sports, politics, gossip, and how if anyone opens the door to this room our careers are in the toilet. We talk mostly about home, until all of a sudden, every time—"Wait a minute. We can use that." Always, comes a story. Always. "Put it on the board," we say. There are dry-erase boards all around us on the walls. One board has the places we order lunch from. One has the places we like to go out to. One board has words that Ray can't pronounce, and the way he actually does pronounce them, which come out of his mouth sounding like *Einsteen* and *mispronunctuation.* Another board is titled "Ray's Surprise Vocabulary" and has some lofty words Ray has actually used correctly in a sentence, like "sharecropper."

Several boards have the name and number of every episode we've done so far, so that when someone has a great idea, someone else can usually point to the board and say, "Number sixty-seven, you moron. We did it already." And then there are the boards with the color-coded ideas. And these colors actually mean something, not like the government with its terror alerts. A certain color indicates this is just an idea. Another color might indicate we got somewhere on that story—we have actual notes on it. And another color means it was turned into an outline already, which means we're doing it. If we've already gotten to the outline stage, it's very rare that we'll throw it out. Steve Skrovan is in charge of the boards, has nice penmanship, and guards these holy scriptures with his life. Quite often he has to physically restrain Lew from varied attempts at humping the boards, and God forbid, smudging them.

In our room, whoever came up with the story idea will usually be assigned to write the outline. Then we'll all go over it and make sure the story (the most important part) works. Then that same writer will write the script, either alone or with help. I'll give notes, they'll give it another shot, and then it belongs to The Room.

We table it, meaning we sit at the table, open the script—page one, I start to read it out loud and we stop at any point to make it better: a better line, a clearer intention, a funnier physical bit, a whole new scene. We may come to the realization that an entire scene is not necessary, or doesn't work, or that the story should go in a whole different direction at this point, and that tabling this script may take longer than we thought, and Jeremy should stop trying to change the ring tone to "Eine Kleine Nachtmusik" on one of those new "cellular telephones" for a second. Whatever happens, the original writer's name will always remain on the script, no matter how much it is subsequently rewritten in The Room. (It is then up to that writer's conscience to show his original draft when applying for other jobs.) But that's the nice way, and our motto at work is Be

Nice. However, in The Writers' Room, when working, nice has no business being there. In The Room, rude and crude is what's called for. Wit and shit, we say.

We all have the ability to be the Room monkey at any given moment, but Lew's the most Simian. He looks like a shorter version of a Jewishy Tom Hanks and he is truly the best at getting us laughing, making fun of us, and just making fun in general. We depend on him. Part of working in The Room is having fun and creating a fun atmosphere so that a little television comedy can come.

All the fooling around is warming up the car. You're getting in the head of trying to be funny, because if somebody told you, "Go in that room and be funny," you'd have to kill yourself. So we don't do that. We go in The Room and everyone is loose because I'm with naturally gifted, funny people. They can't help it; funny things come out, even if they're in a bad mood, like when Lew does a character—for example, the old guy who has to clean up the porno theater whose name is Jizzy. Not everyone outside The Room might appreciate the nuances of this characterization. But we enjoy it. We laugh and laugh at Jizzy's antics and complaints about his particular avenue of show business. We all have bits, and when something bad happens to one of us, well, that's the funniest thing of all.

By the way, we've shared horrible times together.

Lew got called out of The Room once, and when he came back, he told us he had gotten a phone call from his mother that his dad had just had a stroke. And he broke down in The Room.

It was terrible to see a friend in pain, but that's what makes a family. It's not just laughing all the time; it's real people. These are your friends. And we've had all manner of life that you can imagine pass through there in nine years. There is a closeness, and it wasn't until the next day that we made fun of Lew for crying.

Nothing is sacred. Nothing. It can't be. As of this writing, there is a lawsuit pending that's gone all the way to the California Supreme Court—a female writers' assistant was apparently offended by things that were said in The Writers' Room of *Friends.* I'm sorry, but if you got me on that stand, my defense would be, "I'm a comedy writer." As comedy writers, we're going to say every curse known to man, and then we're going to make up some. We're going to insult you and me and everyone we know and don't know, we're going to make sex jokes that make *The Aristocrats* look like the Von Trapps. If you're coming in the comedy room, you're bound to be offended unless you leave Lady Bracknell outside, and we've had plenty of women on board who were filthier than any of us.

I hate that *Friends* lawsuit. They actually printed what was said in The Room. I always thought it was clear that, like Vegas, what went on in The Room, stayed there—the obvious reason being that the sheer idiocy that goes on behind the door could never translate to an outsider. It's very hard to convey to anyone outside the family that no one in that room sees the shit joke as the height of comedy—just the opposite—and the reason we laugh so hard is because of how "wrong" it is. The same goes for every other horrible, insensitive, shocking, moronic, junior high level of wit on display. But it's *our* room. It's only meant as a release to get us going, to warm up the car, so we can then do the best real comedy writing we can do, which is honest, hard work. And this work can't possibly get the respect it deserves in the real world when our stupid (but very necessary) behavior is described out of context, or in context for that matter.

That said, back to our room. Tucker is from Virginia, he's very well educated and he was going to go to law school, but he was a little too funny for law school. He was the most frat-boy of us, and the youngest, yet he's the Scoutmaster now. He sits at one end of the table. If we're in public, he's the one who will say, "Keep your voices down, they can hear you." Usually because we're telling a terrible story about a man who had to take a shit on a train, and Tucker is trying to signal us, "You can't say that in the farmers' market." He's right. The Room should stay in The Room, but sometimes The Room is wherever two or more of us are.

At the other end of the table is Jeremy Stevens, in his sixties, a rarity in today's room. He's bald, white hair around the sides. Sometimes he has a white beard, sometimes he shaves it when his wife can't take it anymore. He has glasses, and is a very amiable-looking fellow. On his worst day, he's amiable. Otherwise he's who Lew calls Effusivo the Clown, because he's the most enthusiastic man we know. "My God, this noodle kugel! Best noodle kugel I ever had. There is no better kugel in the world. You gotta get in on some of this!" as he offers you his shmutzed-up fork.

To Tucker's left is Tom Caltabiano—tall, thin, can eat whatever he wants, as much as he wants, and does not gain an ounce. He's a handsome fellow, he's the only bachelor of the group, he's late every day, and we live vicariously through him. "Please tell us about these dates with beautiful actresses and models." Gorgeous women all the time. All the time. Beautiful, unbelievable. And we just beg for the details of these evenings.

But unfortunately, in this one department, Tom's a gentleman. A gentleman asshole.

He got us all into trouble once when he brought an eighteen-year-old girl to a function that our wives were at. (This, too, ended up as an episode.) The wives asked us, "Why is he dating an eighteen-year-old girl? What could they possibly have to talk about?"

"Maybe they don't have to talk," said Tucker as Every Husband.

You know what, I think she was not even eighteen on the first date, and she didn't tell him that. But in The Room the joke was that he was waiting for her on her birthday—standing with a watch on one hand and her birth certificate in the other.

Poor Tom. He's the happiest guy we know. Standing out by the high school going, "Hello, miss, I'm a comedy writer."

Steve Skrovan is a great stand-up comedian who sat next to

Jeremy for nine years, catching all manner of disease through food crumbs that spewed out of Jeremy's mouth. One of my jobs in New York in the late eighties was scouting comedy clubs in Manhattan for a television show that was going to be, and then wasn't. But I went to comedy clubs all night, every night, different ones all around the city, and I'll tell you something, that was a chore, because there's way more bad comedy than good. Just like there's way more bad everything than good. And I would give the comedians a rating from one to ten with maybe a little comment on my sheet of paper. I did this for months. In 1988 I saw Lew Schneider one night and Steve Skrovan another night. My score sheet still exists. And in 1998, I found it and brought it into The Room. Lew Schneider, in 1988, got a 6.5 on my scale. Steve Skrovan . . . 7.5 on my scale. You still cannot talk to Lew about it without him saying, "I was emceeing that night. It was an off night." He claims to remember the exact night. And Steve, just to bother Lew, ten, twelve years later, he will just look at Lew and go, "7.5."

They're comedians. It's their whole life. But Steve was able to get past it, especially with his higher score. He's also a mature, very well read, very socially active guy. I'm trying to describe what he looks like. I can't. Kind of a Ukranian . . . let's say the most handsome man in the Ukraine.

Lew makes fun of Steve because he wears cargo pants all the time, with the thousands of pockets. And Lew tells him it's not the eighties anymore, and Steve has been known to buy, even though he makes a very good living, used rental cars because they're cheaper. One day, I said in The Room, "Steve's going to be late today. He's actually buying a Prius." And Lew said, "He'll be here, he's just waiting for the guy who's rented it to return it."

And when Steve enters and hears that, he turns to Lew and says, "7.5."

This was the central brain trust. And then there are the guys who came a year or two later. To Steve's left was Mike Royce, another comedian friend of Ray's whose stuff I had read and loved. He's a bald guy, and very thin. He has a wife and two kids. He's got an elfin quality about him, but he's tall. He's a tall elf. (I'm sorry, Mike, but I have to describe you, and it's hard, you big elf bastard.) Other than that, he's absolutely hilarious, a tremendous writer.

Aaron Shore came to us having written on a couple of shows and done odd jobs. He was someone who walked around at Disney World in a period costume in character, part of what Disney called streetmosphere. Yup. He was also a clown. He could ride a unicycle. He did stand-up. He went on Letterman's "Stupid Human Tricks" and snapped a mousetrap on his tongue. The job he had before us was working in a petting zoo. (We had a petting zoo scene in the show once, and Aaron played Fuzzy Acres.) He's a hypochondriac and a conspiracy theorist and a paranoiac and one of the funniest people on God's earth. He's so afraid of getting Alzheimer's that he's thought of the perfect way to deal with it: When he gets old enough, and starts thinking that maybe he's going to get Alzheimer's any time now, he's going to bake a poison pie. He will then put the poison pie into the fridge and leave it there. The day he forgets that he baked the poison pie, he'll eat it and it will be naturally time to go.

To me, that's genius.

He's the one that Ray goes to for health care, because Ray is neurotic, too. Ray will feel under his ribs and say to Aaron, "I've got something on my side here sticking out," and Aaron will say, "Do you have another one like it on the other side?" And Ray will say, "Oh, yeah, I do." And Aaron will say, "Then you're okay."

Two idiots. Two idiots together.

Aaron sits to Lew's right, so he gets jumped on occasionally, and he is also a little gnomish-looking. Also balding, also elfin in charm. Nobody in The Room looks mean or evil. They all look affable and approachable, these guys. None of them looks forbidding or intimidating in any way. We all look like Mister Softees from the ice cream truck.

We're not Mister Softees in The Room, but if another team of comedy writers came to beat us up, we'd probably cry and run away.

And this was basically The Room. We had assigned seats, for much the same reason that Hitchcock had ten identical black suits in his closet—one less thing to think about. And yes, there were always women—some stayed three, four, and five years, but not quite as long as these guys. Comedy seems to be a male-dominated sport; maybe, generally, we are just more monkey. When I read a script, I don't care who wrote it, they're all printed in black and white, and I generally respond to a voice that I can relate to. So I'm looking for any man or woman of any race or religion, as long as they write like an old Jew. Ray is in The Room as much as possible when he's not rehearsing. He's hysterically funny, insightful and astute, and an asset to every script. The few he and I wrote together are among my favorites. We were all talking in The Room one day, and one of us told about an incident where something was overheard at a party on a baby monitor. The young parents had gone upstairs to check on the baby, forgetting that the monitor was on downstairs, and while they were up there, started trashing the guests downstairs. When the couple came back down, the party was obviously over. This seemed like a good area for our show. Would Ray and Debra say something the parents overhear? That seemed the most obvious, and maybe the best—we wouldn't dismiss anything just for its obviousness, it's how you execute the premise that makes the show. But interesting things come from turning ideas around . . . maybe Frank and Marie say something that Ray and Debra overhear on the monitor. Maybe it's not an emotional slight, but some information, a secret. The Room starts buzzing. Hidden money? Hidden money in their basement? Ray and Robert digging around their basement and then it turns out they were set up by the parents as some kind of trust test? Or, what is that money for? Do Frank and Marie have a lot of money and never spend it, and we learn they could have had much nicer lives if they weren't so stingy and crazy? We were always looking for the deeper meaning in every story, something that would have some kind of resonance with the audience, no matter how silly on the surface, and this premise seemed to have some potential. The phone rang, it was time for run-through. That story would have to wait for the moment.

Most days, we're not just writing, since there's a show to actually produce that week, and we have to see how that's coming along. So half the day is working on future shows, and the other half is this week's show. And then there's editing the show we shot two weeks ago, and casting the guest star roles for next week's show, and most important, where's lunch?

We go to run-through, and it's an episode called "The Can Opener," based on another real-life incident where I came home one night after work, and there was no dinner. No problem—Monica was busy with the kids, and I'm fine opening a can of tuna. I like tuna. Monica had bought a new can opener, the kind that cuts around the side of the can, near the top, and removes the whole top of the can that way. I tried it and got an armful of tuna juice. (Monica remembers it as a little drip on my hand.) "Stupid can opener," I remember saying, stupidly. For some reason, this started a fight. "I'm not stupid!" said Monica after a hard day of work with small children to her husband who spent his day hanging with the guys. "I didn't say that. I said the can opener is stupid," I corrected her. "Well, I bought it, and I thought it was good, so why don't you just say I'm stupid!" replied my bride.

This would make a good show, I was already thinking, before my wife stormed upstairs in tears. And so we wrote it with a type of *Rashomon* scenario, where we see Debra's side as she speaks to a sympathetic Robert, and then Ray's side as he talks to an always-on-his-side Marie. And then we get an emotionally invested fight involving everyone in the family, culminating in Frank and Marie's going at it, while Robert needs Pepto-Bismol from all the tension.

When we were writing this one, we thought that what was behind Ray and Debra's fight could be illuminated by Frank and Marie's climactic fight, highlighting the ancient struggle: What do husbands and wives expect from each other in a marriage? What's the understood deal? I go to work, and you tend the cave? How equal is the partnership? Is there a boss? Are some arrangements better left unspoken? We attempted to explore this in the episode, at the end of which, after seeing the pent-up rage of Frank and Marie explode over an old can of fat drippings, Ray and Debra apologize over their spat about the can opener. And we realize, as in all the episodes we did that revolved around inanimate objects (toasters, canisters, vacuum cleaners), it's never really about the can opener.

At run-through we see what the actors have been rehearsing for a few hours that day with the director, and then I get to put in my two cents. Sometimes it's just a question of tweaking a character's attitude in a scene, sometimes the staging needs to be changed drastically for the scene to work, sometimes just a word needs to be emphasized for a joke to score. I give my notes, then I ask my fellow writers if they have anything to add, and decide how best to fix things during these rehearsals. What we try not to do, and what we did do on many other shows I worked on, is go back to The Room, and start rewriting the whole script. It's better to talk to the actors, and try to figure out the difference between what is genuinely a writing problem, an acting problem, and a directing problem. My theater background helps me because I studied these three areas. They're all connected. Many of the people I worked for did not know how to communicate with actors (or regular people, for that matter), and so we'd have to take it out on the script. And that usually meant a bad script and a bad show, and it always meant three in the morning.

With this particular can-opener episode, I remember trying to do these *Rashomon* scenes very carefully, so they would be just exaggerated enough to show that each narrator's point of view was slanted, and yet keep the staging and the dialogue realistic and exactly the same in both versions. This way, it was left to the actors' tone of voice and attitude to demonstrate how the same fight is interpreted by each side. Very nice show, the actors are great, I go home happy that day.

Now, for some reason, that night my wife is very angry with me. I usually can figure out why, but this time, I am truly clueless. I still don't know why, but I soon figure out what it could be. It could be—and I'm only saying *could be*—it could be PMS. This was a rough one. And I would feel terrible for my wife going through the awful physical and emotional turmoil of this time of month if I wasn't so busy feeling terrible for me.

And we fight. And I don't get it. She's usually the sweetest woman in the world. Why, once a month, does she become the Wolfman? And why does she take it out on me? What the hell did I do? Come to think of it, I'll bet the can-opener thing was PMS related. Listen to that yelling, I could use the baby monitor now, so other people could hear . . .

Sometimes, in your darkest hour, God smiles on you.

The next morning, I grabbed Ray and told him about my night. And astonishingly, Ray had had the exact same kind of evening at his house. PMS? You, too? Yes. We have no understanding of women, but we get very excited. "And it's not a baby monitor, it's a tape recorder, you tape her so she can hear what she sounds like, and we make it worse."

And we run into The Room.

Lew stops pretending to hump Steve for a minute and we all jump on this story. We seemed to have hit a nerve here. Soon The Room is a pitiful self-help group of men complaining about how horrible women are at this particular time, and we realize, as with every story, that our jobs require us to explore the other side, our wives' side. There's no fun in that, but we are getting paid. Ray and I decide to write this one together, and within about ten minutes, we have the main story beats all laid out. This is what they mean when they say it writes itself. Of course it never writes itself, but this episode, on this series, with these characters, was meant to be. Because we had taken the time at the start of the series to establish the characters and relationships and we weren't always looking for the quickest, biggest joke, a theatrical machine was now in place to deliver this universal type of story.

The first act would establish that Debra has PMS, which is demonstrated during an afternoon in front of Ray's buddies, his dad, and his brother. The guys can then give us the male point of view, culminating in Frank's speech in which he says that his wife's PMS took over her entire personality and now he just prays "for a comet to come screaming down to earth to bring me sweet relief." Ray decides to help the situation by going to the drugstore and buying Debra some remedies. He then makes the supreme mistake of actually handing them to her. Not only does this not work, but he even angers his mother, who also happens to be a woman, and she slaps him. Debra exits angrily, leaving Ray confused and alone.

The second act finds Ray fighting back. He's had enough of this treatment and he has tape-recorded Debra in an effort to show her that it's not him, it's her, and if she could just hear herself, she'd maybe understand that and maybe try the pills. He plays the tape for Debra, and she hears herself yelling irrationally about lint in the dryer. This tactic, in a surprise to our hero, backfires. Calling Ray a "gigantic ass," Debra storms out of the bedroom and into the kitchen, where Ray is stupid enough to follow. And then comes our Long Day's Journey into Night of PMS. Patty Heaton gives a tour de force performance as a hormonal, desperate housewife, struggling not only with the enemy within, but with Captain Lunkhead, who represents me and Ray and every other married clod. By the end, Ray is once again left alone. There's no happy ending here, he just looks skyward and says, "Come on, comet."

In a recent poll, viewers chose this episode, "Bad Moon Rising," as their all-time favorite of our shows. And I'd just like to say, once again, to my lovely, beautiful, young, svelte wife, "I'm sorry."

Steve has said that his wife will notice a far-off look in his eye when they're having a fight, and Shelly will say, "This is not for the show!" Then Steve will tell her how much a script is worth, and she'll say, "Okay, this one is for the show!"

We have all certainly kept arguments going a bit longer than they might have to go because we need a second act. My wife will watch the show with me when it's broadcast, and sometimes, after Ray has either apologized to Debra for some transgression, or been left miserable by his own selfish motives, my wife will smack my arm and say, "How come you can understand it for television?" Because we control it on television. Ray's wife, Anna, will watch the show with him, and after a Ray-Debra scene, will turn to him and say, "You just talked to her more than you talked to me all week." And Ray's response is, "I have writers there."

And we have wives at home. I'll say right here that our show wouldn't have been half as good without those women—unwittingly providing half the story lines and dialogue for the series. I've always said that whenever I didn't have a story idea, I'd go home and get in a fight with my wife, and that one reason we had to stop doing the show was that if we kept this up, our wives would leave us. And then, according to California state law, they'd get half of everything else.

So, although we were filthy pigs, our wives were always on our minds in The Room, and we tried our best to represent them as well-rounded human beings—human beings we love and readily acknowledge as "the people we work for." The Room is work, sanctuary, hideout, club, dining hall, therapy couch, and if you're as lucky as we were, the happiest place on earth.

9

You Need a Vacation

During our first season, I asked my friend Raymond what he was going to do on his three-month hiatus, and he said, "We like to go to the Jersey Shore."

"That's nice," I said. "How about Europe?"

And Raymond said, "Huh?"

"You've never been to Europe?"

"Nah."

"How about Italy, where your family's from?"

"Nope."

"Why not? Don't you want to go? Why wouldn't you want to go?"

And Raymond said, "I'm . . . not really interested in other cultures."

Even his own. Even his own culture. So I thought, *This might be a good episode.* You send him over to Italy as Ray Romano, and you bring him back as Roberto Benigni after he's been transformed by the magic of traveling, and especially by Italy, my favorite place on earth.

It took four years of the show's being successful to ask CBS to sponsor our one-hour Italy show. It would be the premiere of season five, and one of the perks of this little scam was that I had to go over and scout locations as soon as we wrapped season four. I took some of our production team, I took my lovely wife, and I spent five days getting inspired. And I did—we found wonderful spots in Rome, and a little town about forty minutes north of Rome, called Anguillara, on the Lago di Bracciano, and these places—the gelato stand, the outdoor cafés, the lake itself, the streets, the people we met—actually started dictating the content of the script I was writing. We had a great time, but I was still working. I needed a real vacation, and I realized I hadn't had one in more than five years, since before I started working on the show.

So here was my good idea: Before shooting began on the Italy episode in August, I'd bring my family over to Italy and spend a few days in Venice and then Florence before heading to Rome. I'd spend some time with them there, and then they'd go home just as we started our week of production.

It would be Monica; Ben, six; Lily, three; and me. And then—and I'm not quite sure how this happened—also joining us on our real vacation would be my parents, Max, seventy-seven, and Helen, seventy.

Yes. Life was about to imitate art, which hadn't been filmed yet. But by now we all know the series and where it came from and where it usually goes.

Our very first night, in Venice—we're staying at a lovely hotel, we're getting ready to go out for dinner, and there's a knock at the door. I open it to find my father standing in his underpants in the hallway.

"Dad, we're not at home," I say, sensing the long, internationally embarrassing road ahead.

"Mom fell," says my father.

I run over to the next room and find my mother sitting on the bed in a towel, holding another towel up to her face. There's blood.

She had slipped getting out of the tub and fell on her face on the beautiful Venetian marble floor. The hotel staff comes right up and whisks her and Monica away by ambulance boat to the hospital.

Now, I make fun of Mom professionally. I could actually put that on the tax forms as my occupation. But she came back from the hospital, twelve stitches later, a broken cheekbone, holding a giant ice bag on her face, and insisted that we were not going to miss dinner. We didn't and we had a great time, and she was fantastic the entire trip, an absolute trouper—far stronger and more fun to be with than I would have been if I hurt my pinky.

Venice is wonderful for kids, with the water streets and the filthy pigeons. The whole place is like the It's a Small, Small World ride, except everyone waving is Italian. And your kids will walk anywhere, as long as they are eventually walking toward gelato or pizza. My vacation was not ruined by my kids, my wife, or even my parents. It was ruined by show business.

The network and studios had not made deals with all of the actors yet for the coming season, and shooting was to start in Rome in a week. Monica remembers our beautiful trip to Italy like this: Everyone would be sitting in a restaurant that I had researched and reserved months before, eating a delicious dinner, while I paced outside on the sidewalk on a cell phone, yelling, "Make the deal!" to various agents and network and studio people. None of these people seemed aware that this episode of our show in Italy was my passion, and that they were jeopardizing it. In Florence, as we were crossing the Ponte Vecchio, my cell phone rang. This time it was a network executive. "We've gone over the budget for this thing, and the ratings don't really justify the expense."

Shooting was four days away.

"Um, what would you like us to do?" I asked, stopping dead on one of the world's more glorious bridges.

"Go through the script and see what you really don't need" was his suggestion. This was literally suggesting that I start ticking off the Italian locations that weren't necessary to shooting a show about, and in, Italy. "Any colors we should do without?" I wanted to ask, but instead I said, "Um, I'll try to be as frugal and responsible as possible. But at a certain point we're either doing the Italy show or we're not. Italy is what we're in Italy for."

"Well, take a look at it, see what you can do," came the directive, as if the network hadn't had the script for months.

I didn't change anything. Except the way I understood a vacation was supposed to be. This wasn't it. My family was mad at me for obvious reasons, and I was mad at the business part of show business. It wasn't until the night before we started shooting that I finally was able to yell, coerce, beg, and plead with all the parties concerned to ensure that all the actors would be on location in Rome the next day.

Once we were all together, we did our jobs and had fun doing them. Our longtime wonderful director, Gary Halvorson, got some achingly beautiful shots of all the places that were supposed to be budgetary cuts. Combining all these things that I loved—the show, the people on the show, the people of Italy, the food, the sights—was a dream, and I was very proud of the result; it was our little movie.

Of course, what happened in the episode to Raymond actually happened to Ray the person. He fell in love with Italy, and his eyes were opened. So was his mouth—every night after work, we'd have a terrific dinner, then he'd want gelato. And we'd walk, then he'd have to have pizza at this place we hadn't tried yet. And we'd walk, of course stumbling onto another gelateria we hadn't pillaged yet. Every night. Ray would walk anywhere as long as it ended up at pizza or gelato.

And from there, he had a vacation with his family in Sicily, where his wife's parents are from, and actually relived some of the same situations as in the show we'd just shot. When we returned home with the footage, we filmed all the interior scenes on our stage with an audience, rolling back the Italian exterior scenes for them in the right places of our story. Quite often, if a joke goes badly on shoot night, and a writer has fought for that joke all week, it is customary to turn to the writer and ask, with as much subtle sarcasm as one can muster during the dead air where a laugh ought to be, "Did you get what you wanted?"

I have to say that when all was said and done, with all the mishegoss that went into the production of that hour, the Italy show was exactly what I wanted. If you think it's too sentimental in spots, I apologize. All I can say when someone isn't crazy about a particular episode is, "That's okay. They can't all be for you. I like some more than others, too." And then I cry into my pillow.

We were on to season six and we did twenty-five episodes that season; it was a very nice season, writing and rewriting, casting and editing, rehearsing and shooting, eating and drinking. But even though I loved my job, I still hadn't had a vacation. I was starting to understand what people meant when they said, "I'm tired." It was now going on six years, and I vowed that I was going to do this, have a friggin' vacation—no work, just great family time, relax, have fun, that's all. Lew suggested a place in Mexico he had checked out that seemed perfect for families—in fact, he was going with his family during Christmas week and we should come. It was a tropical beach location (I had never done that—always a city type), everything was included, it was a good deal, it sounded great, and we booked it. I couldn't wait for that week to arrive. I hadn't gone away like this for so long, I almost felt guilty for going. I know that sounds crazy, but I had forgotten how to let go. But I did let go, and I finally convinced myself that I deserved this. What follows is from my e-mail journal to my friends and family back home of that magical time . . .

"All-Inclusive Resort," four A.M.

It's hot. I'm hot and sticky. The air-conditioning in the room turns the sticky into clammy. The kids love it here already. Monica and everyone else I can see are having a good time, too. Their attitudes are great. I've been informed that mine stinks. The airport yesterday, for security as well as holiday reasons, was jammed—long lines. The flight was kid-filled (and so screaming-and-crying-filled). We land on an airstrip that only makes me think of the movie *Traffic,* and I'm sure that all the baggage handlers and workers have other, more lucrative, jobs. And it's really hot. Over ninety degrees, and very humid. So the first thing you want to do is get on a bus for an un-air-conditioned forty-minute drive through poverty to a resort. As we ride, a large French woman is on the mike in the bus, telling us about the required wristbands: "You have paid a lot for your meals, so you don't want some guy coming up from the beach and eating with you for free." She also tells us about the "excursions"—fishing, shopping(!), and so on, which cost extra. She tells us about meal times, which will be seven A.M., twelve, and seven P.M. Snacks (and alcohol, except for beer and wine) are extra, so you will have to buy books of tickets. As soon as we get to the club, we are told that we will be told the exact same things by another French lady.

We arrive at "All-Inclusive Resort," and debus. The entire staff is lined up and clapping for us and the other busloads as we walk through them. Music plays. Fruit punch is served. (Yes, I'm thinking of Guyana.) The wristband is snapped on. The head French lady speaks. One representative from each family must go to the conference room now and give a credit-card imprint. Then you get your room keys, an "All-Inclusive Resort" credit card, and towel cards (one per family member—give the card, get a towel). A staffer takes us to the giant pile of luggage in the parking lot so we can identify our stuff, then tells us that the luggage will be brought to the front of our building, then shows us to our rooms.

The rooms are more like cabanas. We are on the first floor, and would have a nice ocean view if not for the bars on the windows, which aren't just bars but include big squares of iron. After getting into shorts, Lew—who, with his family, is next door—and I retrieve the bags, which involves shlepping and stairs. We have four pretty big bags, because we're staying here a week.

The French lady also tells us to be at the "theater" at six-thirty for an orientation, about an hour from now. There's no clock in the room, just like Vegas. I unpack and see about connecting to the Internet—it'll be about twelve pesos a minute (a dollar something), which doesn't seem so bad. I'm given my own dial-out code so I can be easily charged. We head over to the main building, which has the dining hall, reception, an "All-Inclusive Resort" shop, excursions office, an open-air bar, and the open-air theater. We meet Evan and Evelyn Plimpton and their three kids there—we know them from the kids' school. They had asked what we were doing for the holidays, then booked the same trip. They had taken a regular Alaskan Airlines flight and are in a much better mood.

Dinner is a big buffet with a big selection of food. It's not bad, but it's not really good, either. The dining room is open-air, too, and the heat doesn't help, we're all sweating into our meal. After dinner, it's time for a show in the theater—"Stars of the World," which features "All-Inclusive Resort" employees. I can't take any more, so I return to the room by myself. It's weakly air-conditioned, but there's a TV. CNN has the story of the guy on an American Airlines flight from Paris to Miami who tried to light his shoe on fire because he apparently had C4 plastic explosives in it. Maybe I should've tried that. Monica and the kids return, having had a great time. I am the stick in the mud that is "All-Inclusive Resort."

I have a mostly sleepless night. All this would be so much more bearable if I wasn't sweating. I think nonstop about going home. We have such a nice house. I want to cut the plastic "All-Inclusive Resort" meal band off my wrist.

Day 2

Lew and I go to the bar for a watered-down Glenfiddich (a scam involving ten blue tickets and a red ticket). Then Ben and his friend

Bobby want to play in the video game room—five dollars for twenty-five minutes. Lily dances with the discoing crowd around the pool, then mercifully wants to go back to the room, so I volunteer. Lily and I have fun watching cartoons with weak air-conditioning.

Day 3

Wrenched my back a bit yesterday. Would love a massage, but there's no spa here. So the excursions people said they'd set something up with someone from the outside. Hasn't worked out so far. Had b'fast, Monica and Ben went on their "swim with dolphins" excursion, and I dropped Lily off at camp, amid much crying and begging (her, not me), until I got her on the trampoline. That she likes, so it's easier for me to go work out, which I do, and now I'm back in the room, watching CNN, TNT, typing this, and waiting to hear about a massage. There is actually a hut on the beach they call a massage center, but it's so hot, the last thing you want is someone touching you out there. Yes, I'm complaining a lot, and while I dislike myself for it, I'd be very pleasant at home. After lunch (chewy chicken tacos), spent a couple of hours in the ocean with Ben and had a good time. Lew is actually learning the trapeze. It's good to have a skill to fall back on. There is bad Christmas music piped in around the pool for all to enjoy in the ninety-eight-degree weather. My masseuse arrives late and she has the hands of a man who splits wood for a living—dry and chapped—so it's not unlike one of those salt rubs with the added, disgusting knowledge that this isn't salt.

Then a huge "All-Inclusive Resort" Christmas Eve buffet (every meal is a buffet, by the way—the whole place is like a Chuck E. Cheese cruise ship) with huge lines for the grilled lobster, which are not "top of the tank." The other food's not bad, but I've really had enough of this cavernous, loud dining room/feeding frenzy. And there's nothing like the sight of a hugely fat guy walking around the dining rooms with his shirt wide open and his belly hanging over his shorts like a wheelbarrow load of pork, while eating. After dinner, more Euro disco crap led by a screaming French "entertainer" at poolside. Lew does a good imitation of him: "Body pump!" Everyone loves the dancing. Evan had a good line after seeing my face there—"Wait till the third ghost visits you tonight."

Yes.

Next, the evening's entertainment—the staff presents "Dances from Around the World." First up: Scotland, with twenty guys marching around in kilts for a half hour. Lew and I hit the bar for some more watered-down drinks. Not drunk at all—they actually *are* watering down the liquor! Is this not the equivalent of taking away one's pet rat in solitary? Back at the Old Globe, the country of Transvestia must be up, because there's a drag queen or two jumping around for the children of all ages. Lily has passed out, flat on the floor, like a girl at a frat house, so it must be time to go back to the room. I have accepted that I'm here; that my family loves it, and that I will go home again, after many, many more groundhoglike days.

Day 4—A Christmas Memory

Ben and I had an eight-thirty swim in the ocean this morning—the boy could live in there, he loves it so much. Then b'fast, another workout for me—I have never worked out every day before, which tells you something, then a shower. By the way, I believe you can tell the soul of a hotel by the water pressure in the shower. It can have the fancy lobby, nice linens, good service, but if the water pressure stinks, so does the hotel. Guess what the water pressure is like here? Like a drooling drunk. But this place doesn't mislead you by having the lobby, linens, or service, either.

Then out to the pool for the "All-Inclusive Resort" Christmas parade—hot and sticky as a broken New York subway in August, dozens of guest children march around the pool in face paint and costumes, following a poor staffer in a full chipmunk costume complete with suffocating head. The music—more Euro disco. Then everyone rushes to the balcony to see Santa Claus parasailing onto the beach. We lose a couple of towels in the frenzy, and this is bad, because a family of four starts with four towels, which you can get laundered in exchange for the towel card, which you hold on to until you need another towel. If, by the end of your stay, you don't return a combination of your original allotment of towels or cards, you are fined $22. Per towel. So it's only Wednesday, and we're down a couple of towels. Theft has crossed my mind.

Santa sets up shop in the theater and all thousand adults wait to get a photo of their kid on his sweaty lap, and each kid gets an "All-Inclusive Resort" hat or plastic blow-up float. Then lunch buffet, then a nap, then a couple more hours in the ocean with Ben and friends. The water is nice and warm, but I noticed a strange rash on my legs.

Now, we learn of a guy whom Lew has played tennis with the past couple of mornings. He's a fifty-one-year-old guy from New York with a wife, a twelve-year-old son, and a fifteen-year-old daughter and he was in a doubles tournament this afternoon. He finished his game and had a heart attack. It's horrible. We see the medics rushing over, but we hear his heart's been stopped for more than forty minutes, and as they wheel him away, there's still no pulse. We hear later that he didn't make it.

Jokes included were: This is now officially a death camp. . . . And, Quick, get his towel. I'm here all week.

Dinner was a Mexican buffet. I can't remember eating breakfast, lunch, and dinner in the same room every day since before starting preschool. Even Ben says he's bored with the same room every meal. That's my boy. Chicken mole was good. Pork skins in green sauce were less so. If the guy hadn't died on the tennis court . . .

After dinner, Lew and I retire to the hot, open-air bar. Tonight I'll have shots of vodka. As we are drinking, Evelyn Plimpton crosses the bar holding her youngest (but not small) child, Irwin, and he suddenly pukes a bucketful all over her and the barroom floor to the strains of "The Macarena." Paradise.

Day 5

The kids fell asleep in bed with us last night, so this morning, of course, we woke up in a wet bed. At breakfast we hear another story from yesterday: While the man was dying on the tennis court, elsewhere in Xanadu a teenage girl was stung by a bee and went into the kind of shock (anaphylactic?) where you cannot breathe. Her parents try to call for help, but the medical "staff" was busy beating on the dead man's chest over at center court. The father of the girl runs to the infirmary (far) to find no one there, so he goes to the medicine chest—he's a psychiatrist, so he has a medical background—but the medicine chest is locked. He breaks the thing open, grabs a hypodermic needle and medicine, runs back, gives his daughter the injection . . . and saves her life.

I can honestly say I'm having an incredible time here. I want to go home. When I say this to people, they think I'm kidding. I'm not. I've become a misanthrope. My wife is not thrilled with my demeanor. She wants to know what I've been writing about. I just showed her, and she left the room, saying, "You're lucky you're funny."

Tonight the grown-ups were going to go out to eat, but after hours of trying to get a straight answer from the resort's bozos about child care, which turns out to be easy and all-inclusive, unless you go out at night (when else?), we finally just gave up and ate, once again, amid the hot, the crying, the screaming, and the fat. But it was Asian night. What looked like tofu was actually rectangles of cream cheese, and you could have a tuna roll made with the tuna fish from a can with the mayo mixed in for those of us sushi beginners. This was the night to have gone out. Even Monica got fed up with the management tonight, so I thought the timing was right for "You want to go home tomorrow?" She gave me the blessing, and I immediately asked the front desk about switching our flights, which, of course, is impossible. Forget it, we're here till Saturday. But we're eating in a goddamn restaurant tomorrow. During this, the two kids whose father died yesterday pass us. Lew offers his condolences (he had played tennis with the father and son that morning) and both kids burst into tears. Truly heartbreaking.

But I don't want to make this place sound like it's completely devoid of fun.

Have I mentioned the mosquitoes?

Day 6

Signed up for tennis today.

Day 6, Continued

Actually, since it wasn't excruciatingly hot, took a bike ride this morning off campus. They do charge you for the bike rental—what exactly *is* included in the "all-inclusive" fee? They showed me a route to the bike trail through the jungle swamp and said it was a total of six miles and would take an hour, so I rented the bike for an hour, and it took me a half hour. Is this because I am a world-class athlete, or is this another case of "watering down"? It's all in my new book, *The Paranoiac's Guide to Vacationing.* The trail was nice, though—paved, and there was a lookout point over the swamp where I saw a white crane, and something moving in the tall grass—a lion? A wild boar? It was a cow. And there was another and another. I'm an idiot. But for one glorious half hour, I was a free idiot. You could almost say that my bike ride was worth the trip, in which case, you'd be the idiot. Didn't see the promised crocodiles either, but there was a floating empty two-liter Pepsi bottle, and across the road, one of those beachside shack/bars like where Albert Finney drank himself to death in *Under the Volcano.*

Hmmmm.

Monica and Lew's wife, Liz, have conversations here that go like this—"Are those your towels or my towels? I had three, no two, but one might still be with the kids, but wait, here's a towel card, or is that yours?" I never want to see, or use, a towel again.

The wives have also arranged for a couple of babysitters for tonight, because we will be eating out or I will be going cannibal, and last night was so frustrating because there's a "club" that charges twenty dollars per kid to sit them in front of the VCR for the evening, when the kids would rather run around, play Ping-Pong, drink booze, whatever. The wives figured they could just hire a couple of staffers for the night to let the kids do what they want. I just found out, and they don't know it yet, but "All-Inclusive Resort" doesn't want the liability. Nor will they allow you to hire an outside babysitter; you must use Siesta Club. They do seem very protective of the children, don't they? Maybe they could be a little more protective of the middle-aged folks who are encouraged, out of boredom, to exert themselves beyond capacity in this sweltering hell.

Another tropical depression washes over me as I enter the dining hall this afternoon—what's this one? Lunch? It is my seventeenth meal in a row in this room, and I look around to find the now familiar characters in my vacation dreamland. There's Fatso Openshirt, and there are The Long Island Matching Fake Boob Mommies (one of them likes the white-lipstick look on her collagened mouth), there's Mister Hasn't Been Told This Isn't the Home So He Walks Around the Dining Room in His Bathrobe and Slippers, and there's the rest of the nice poor suckers, too, me included (without the nice), shuffling around, amid the crying and the whining, looking for a way to eat as much of our money's worth in meat, cheese, and stale pastries as possible. Two more days.

At four-thirty, Monica, Lew, and Liz are going for a horseback ride at sunset on the beach ($). I talked with someone who did this on Tuesday, because I was considering going. She said, "Oh, you're going? Listen, just look to the left, not the right."

Why? "Because the ocean's on the left, but they take you on the public beach, so there's lots of, y'know . . . trash."

So I will not be joining my bride on her gallop through the garbage this evening. I will await her return and then whisk her away, by motor coach, to a restaurant by the sea, with a wine list, while the children enjoy the glories of Siesta Club.

I tell Lew and Monica about the babysitting situation when they return from their horsey ride (they enjoyed it, by looking left). Monica is somewhat stunned at the news, and Lew, of all people, flips out—cursing and threatening to take a golf club to one of the rooms (though not his own) upon checkout. He's just now reached his fed-up point and joined the real club. But we work out an arrangement with the Plimptons' au pair; she will watch all eight kids for a couple of hours, armed with DVDs, TV, snack money, and more money. And we're bustin' outta here!

We take cabs to a scenic spot built on a cliff that I have cross-referenced as having excellent food. I hate to spoil the tone of this journal, but we had a great time—good food, good wine, laughs, dessert, a European-like view, and drinkable coffee. For me this night out has been a taste of what I've been missing—the equivalent of the scene in *Midnight Express* when the girlfriend visits the guy from behind the glass. The ride takes us to a lovely if somewhat touristy town with a promenade and lots of shops and restaurants. You know you're staying in a lousy place when you pass a Radisson and go, "Ohhhhhhh."

Day 7

If you hadn't had a real vacation in six years, and someone told you you were going to have one for a week in a hot, muggy place, with lots of children and less than great facilities, accommodations, service, and water pressure, and that you'd be eating in the same un-air-conditioned buffet hall for twenty-one meals in a row, you could now say, "I know the schmuck who did that."

After a mostly sleepless night and cereal for breakfast with the soy milk that the "chef" holds for me in what may be the resort's only refrigerator, we think it might be fun to send Lily to camp and take Ben on a bike ride through that preserve with the Schneiders. So after signing up ($) and then taking that receipt up to the slow fellow who gives you the bikes, we find there is no bike that is small enough for Ben, who, whatever other faults he may have—like not handling disappointment very well yet—is not abnormally small. He tries, and we try to make it work, as it gets hotter and hotter, but the bikes are just too big, and he's terrified and frustrated because he really wants to go. Instead, he gets to see his friends go on without him. And we're off to a beautiful start of the day. I take him back to the room, and soothe both our nerves with a shot of cartoons. I'll probably be presented with a three-thousand-peso cartoon bill upon departure. Speaking of departure, our flight is 4:45 P.M. tom'w, so what time do they want you to get your luggage up to the parking lot? 7:30 A.M. I am so dreading this. Given the awfulness of our arrival at the camp (and that was when they were trying to make the place look good), I am imagining a final grab of the wallet and kick in the ass to send us suckers on our way.

Lew returned from the bike trip—Leo (who's not much bigger than Ben) got about twenty feet down the "All-Inclusive Resort" driveway before falling over and cutting himself. Every night in the dining hall has been a theme—Italian night, Asian night, French night, Mexican night. Tonight's theme in the dining hall is International night, otherwise known as leftovers. We're going out again, but we're going to try it with the kids tonight because of . . . well, pity. After lunch, worked out, and went in the ocean with Ben, where a kid threw up his lunch right next to me. So we went to the pool. Leaving the pool, I stepped on and got stung by a bee. No, I'm not kidding.

I thought, *Well, I've never been in anaphylactic shock; it's got to be a better place than "All-Inclusive Resort," so let's go.* No such luck, though, just the physical manifestation of pain from a week of here. Evelyn Plimpton got the stinger out of my foot, so I promised not to kill her next time our paths crossed.

Just got back from dinner with the Schneiders and the kids—beautiful view, the kids were well behaved (Lily slept through the whole thing), and the best margaritas we ever had. I didn't even mind that the food was so-so (everything had cheese on it, even the fish). I sleep now, I'm loopy and I go home tomorrow.

Day 8—Exodus

When we left the restaurant last night, Lew and I took one cab with Ben and Jake on the fifteen-minute drive back to camp. Monica and Liz were going to follow with the rest of the kids. I fell asleep soon after writing my last installment, and woke up a little later to discover that Monica wasn't back yet. I knocked on Lew's door (waking him up out of his drunken stupor)—no Liz, either. We gave it another fifteen minutes and began trying to call the restaurant, which was a nightmare of wrong phone number information for about half an hour, all the while I'm thinking of nothing but Mexican ditches. Two hours after we left them, the girls come in—"We took the funicular!" (The restaurant has one that goes down to the beach from the hilltop.) And after storing up the yelling for a week, I sort of lost it. The F word was used liberally. Liz said to me later, "I hope we're still friends."

I'd say the vacation was now complete, no?

After waking Monica up later to yell some more, I went back to sleep, and now await release. It will be hard to resist singing "Born Free."

The staff lines up to give us its obligatory musical clapping send-off as we get on what has to be one of the more pleasurable bus rides of my life, because it is on this bus that I gnaw the "All-Inclusive Resort" meal bracelet off my wrist like a fox in a bear trap.

Four hours later. On the plane now, on the computer. Forgot to mention that it fell about one foot, in its case, at the airport and hasn't worked right since. I have not made any of this up.

If one thing has stuck with me from this trip, it's the death of the tennis guy. The family, after having to endure legalities such as a foreign autopsy, couldn't leave for a couple of days after. Apparently, the fifteen-year-old daughter was inconsolable because after the man's tennis match (with his son), he said to her, "Come here and give me a hug." And she waved him off because she was with friends. And that was it.

Everyone has made up after last night and the Funicular Incident, we're all like family again, and as I sit here, crammed into the center seat of three across, among the screaming and the crying, I'm grateful. Because "All-Inclusive Resort" was not my idea. I believe it was Lew's.

10

Ahhh, Work

After such a vacation, who wouldn't look forward to the office? I thank that Mexican resort for making me appreciate what I had: a good job, good food for lunch every day, and good friends (except for Lew). And on our show, we had great hours, with air-conditioning. We were getting a nice reputation. One of Lew's friends, another writer, asked him, "How are things at *Raymond,* where all the desks are made of chocolate?"

A few other highlights of season five: Right after "Italy" was show number 100 (written by Lew), in which, to demonstrate how intrusive family can sometimes be, Marie and Frank drove their car through the front wall of Ray and Debra's house. We were spending the money that year. We did that stunt live in front of the audience—the car was pulled on a cable, crashed through the set, and we actually had Doris and Peter in the car for the ride (saved money on stunt people).

Our Thanksgiving episode that season, entitled "Fighting In-Laws" (Kathy Stumpe), contained a bit of stage business that we've been told people enjoy: Debra, angry at Ray because her parents are fighting for a change, drops the Thanksgiving turkey on the floor. To give you some idea how these things evolve, we had in the script that she drops it on the floor and then puts it into the oven. When we got to rehearsal, we saw that the turkey was somewhat slippery, so we had Patty drop it, try to pick it up, drop it again, try again, drop it once more, and then yank open the oven door, throw the turkey in, kick the door shut, and storm off. Come shoot night, Patty was doing the bit, and because we were now using real butter and the floor got covered in butter and turkey grease, she actually lost her footing a little and had to struggle just to stay upright. This slipping around made the bit, and it's one of the biggest laughs and cheers we ever got. You can see Ray standing in the kitchen, holding for the laugh after her exit, before he finally says, "I always wondered where the flavor came from."

"Humm Vac" (Lew Schneider) was the episode in which Marie finally removes the plastic slipcover from her sofa, and the men in her life get their first feel of naked couch fabric. What follows was a lovely pantomime from Ray, Brad, and Doris—the boys are happy to have the awful slipcover gone, but they must, under Marie's extremely watchful eye, be very careful not to smudge this now unprotected sofa. Raymond makes the mistake of eating a potato chip while sitting next to his mother on the precious couch, and he's about to wipe his hands on the fabric when he feels Marie's eyes bearing down on him. Tucker came up with the idea in rehearsal of Ray, unable to wipe his hands anywhere safely, winding up just sitting there, turning his palms upward toward heaven in supplication.

"The Canister" (by outside writer David Regal) was the very next show, and was an out-and-out farce. What grounded this episode for us was that while going over the script in The Room, we found a spot for some unexpected emotion. Marie comes over and asks for her beloved canister back from Debra; Debra says she returned it. Marie is sure she didn't and asks her to look for it. Debra blows up at her—Marie actually apologizes and exits. Ally enters from upstairs with the canister. After trying to dispose of it several times (it keeps coming back like a corpse in a horror movie), Debra finally tries to hide the canister in Marie's own house so that she doesn't have to admit to Marie that Marie was right and she was wrong. (You with me?) Frank catches Debra while she is trying to plant the canister in Marie and Frank's living room. "Give your soul to God, 'cause your ass belongs to Marie," says Frank.

Just then Marie enters and, panicking, Debra thrusts the canister into Frank's hands. Marie turns on Frank, and Frank, rather than just handing the canister back to Debra and telling the truth, lies, and says he was hiding the canister from Marie because he thought it'd be funny. Marie explodes at Frank in an angry tirade and storms off. Debra asks Frank why he did that for her, and Frank says, "Because . . . you're like my daughter."

I apologize again for the sentimentality, but these revealing moments (never a whole "very special episode") make the show for me, just as much as, and contributing to, the laughs. No matter how seemingly silly the episode was, we felt the need to tie each one down to some sort of emotional underpinning, something that would resonate with the viewer after the show was over. I also want you to know that these deeply resonating emotional moments were how we felt about our work and about one another. Such feelings are what runs underneath families, not coming out too often in most, but it's what obviously keeps them together.

Loyalty is hard to come by, but we had a wonderful group that stuck together, especially the crew. Camera-blocking day was usually our third day of rehearsal, and the first time the crew (camera operators, sound guys, and so on) would see the show. It was always a joy to hear them laugh, and a very reassuring sign that maybe we wouldn't bomb this time. No star trips were tolerated—talent and power do not excuse you from being a human being, and our whole staff got along terrifically. (This was not always the case on some shows. On one particular little-known series, we were at rehearsal, and the lead actor was having trouble executing a physical bit. I watched for a while as the director and executive producer and the actor tried to figure it out. Finally I said, "I might have an idea. What if you went behind the couch first—" and the actor cut me off and said, "I might have an idea, why don't you go fuck yourself?" And so I did. And that gentleman never got the bit right. And I believe his TV show went away because he was so impolite.) I had seen abuse, had been abused, and we would have none of it. My friend Alan brought me a sign from a Catskills resort: BE NICE—A HOMAWACK TRADITION, and that sign hung backstage over our craft service table for many years, until someone stole it.

As season six began, I started to wonder how long we could keep going. I was positive that we had maybe one more season left after this before the story well ran dry, and besides, since *The Mary Tyler Moore Show* (the standard-bearer) lasted seven years and then got out on *its* terms, I thought we shouldn't push our luck.

Monica and I went to Ben's first-grade class one day with my parents, who were in town visiting. The occasion was that the children of the class were going to read stories that they themselves had written, and all the parents had come to see them. It was very cute. One little girl got up and told the story of "The Lion Who Had Chicken Pox." Apparently, this lion had chicken pox and went to his mother, who took the lion to the pharmacy for chicken pox cream, which cleared it up, the end, adorable. She had even drawn pictures. A little boy got up on the story-reading chair at the front of the class and told us all the tale of "Escape from the Blue Planet," a marvelous science fiction yarn, also with pictures, about a rocket ship getting stuck and then finding the gas to go on. A delight from start to finish. Ben Rosenthal was next, and he walked to the chair, hopped up on it, opened the book that he had written, and began to read "The Angry Family."

The entire classroom full of parents turned and looked at us as Ben continued . . . "The daddy was mad at the mommy." He showed the picture he had drawn. "The mommy was mad at the daddy." Picture. "They were both very mad at the children." Picture. I was mortified. But in the next split second I asked myself, *How lucky am I to have a child who writes for my television show?*

"The Angry Family" was our season opener, and if you look at the end credits you'll see "Special Thanks: Ben Rosenthal," which I wanted to do because I will not be giving him any money.

Writer Jennifer Crittenden came in to work one day complaining about a sculpture her mother had given her that looked like a part of the female anatomy. A lower part. It was a small sculpture, maybe about six inches high, but Jennifer was so embarrassed by it she didn't want it in her house. She asked us how she could tell her mother that. "Well, the first thing you could tell her is that we're doing this story on *Raymond,*" we said. And this story of "Marie's Sculpture" came together pretty quickly in The Room. Of course, it couldn't be a six-inch sculpture, we're on television and in front of an audience; we needed a three- or four-foot sculpture that was easily seen. And then I remembered, out in front of the Rockland County, New York, courthouse, there was a huge, modern type of abstract sculpture that was quite infamous for looking like . . . exactly what we were looking for. I had to show the prop department. I called my parents. They were having dinner.

"Hi, Ma, listen, could you or Dad go down to the courthouse tomorrow and take a picture of the sculpture? I need it for the show."

"Sure," said my mother and she turned to my father. You could hear the clinking silverware and eating in the background. "Max, go down to the courthouse tomorrow and take a picture of the vagina sculpture."

The clinking stopped.

In the background, you could hear my father say, in as Jewish a way as possible, "The what?"

"The vagina sculpture, Max. At the courthouse. Philip needs you to take a picture of the vagina sculpture at the courthouse."

Another moment, and my father says, "There's a vagina sculpture at the courthouse?"

"Yes, Max," says my mother, centuries of marital exasperation coming through. "The vagina sculpture. Everyone calls it the vagina sculpture, Max. It's the vagina sculpture, the vagina. CAN'T YOU SEE IT'S A VAGINA, MAX?"

And my father says, "What do I know from vaginas?"

This was one of the few times we didn't use actual dialogue from home in the show itself. We never said the word "vagina" or any other descriptive word in this episode, and that may be why we never got a standards and practices note. It was all in the eye of the beholder, you filthy people. My favorite line in that show comes when Marie is finally told what everyone else in the show, including nuns, sees in her abstract sculpture. She looks at it again with new eyes, takes a long moment, and says, "My God, I'm a lesbian." Lew came up with that line. I almost wanted to forgive him for Mexico, but where's the fun in that?

One of my friends who'd been toiling in sitcom land for a while went home and yelled at his parents, "Why couldn't you be crazy like Phil's family?" I got lucky. I had that family. But other people have something else. Like a mother who actually makes her daughter a vagina sculpture. Whenever I speak on panels, the Fruit-of-the-Month scene comes up because it was in the pilot and set the tone. You all have a Fruit-of-the-Month scene, I tell them. And now I tell you: You all have that insane moment, or year, or life that only happened to you. And if you're smart you'll write it down. "Write what you know" didn't become a saying for no reason.

As for performance, we play every scene in the show for drama. This is really happening. We're not trying to be funny. We're 100 percent serious when we say, "I can't talk anymore, there's too much fruit in the house." Marie means it. It's absurd, but it's only funny because it's played for real.

The best note I ever received as an actor I got when I was doing too much on stage—you know, trying to be funny. My speech teacher from college, Mrs. Estelle Aden, came backstage and took me aside. She said, "It was very good, but let them come to you."

"Let them come to you" means just be. Don't playact at being the character, just be the character. Just be. Just live. Don't push. So that applies to everything. It's one of those notes that applies to everything in life. Let them come to you. Just be. Just be you. Don't push; they're going to like you at the party. It's going to be fine. We tend to like people who are real and believable and are like us. It doesn't mean you don't do anything, but you don't push it. You don't show the audience that you're doing an action. "Look how I brush my hair away from my face so slowly to show I'm really interested in what the other actor is saying"—you just *are* interested. Same in writing. Same if you wear too much makeup and your clothes are too revealing. You might attract a certain type of man that way. But that's only because he knows that you're easy and desperate. But I don't want to talk about my wife. The point is: Let them come to you, and they will. I never forgot that note as an actor, a writer, a director, or a showrunner. We're not pushing it in your face; we're just doing it. We're just letting it be, man.

Buster Keaton had no expression on his face. He was hilarious because we projected onto that face as if it were a screen—and with subtlety and music and camera angles and the proper setup, he was letting us know what he was thinking, even though his face wasn't moving. My favorite thing in comedy is a straight face. Jack Benny had it; Walter Matthau had it; Carroll O'Connor had it. Everyone in our cast had it. The deadpan look. To me the golden key in comedy is: They know what you're thinking. That's why we take so many pauses in the show. So that the look will get the laugh because the audience, once the characters have been established, knows what Robert is thinking when Ray gets a big homemade cake from Mom. And we know what Debra is thinking. And Frank. And Marie and Raymond.

We write it that way, the actors do it that way, and then we have to stage and film it that way. In the staging, a moment like Ray's expounding on the wonders of marriage to Robert and then Frank's saying, "I would like a minute for rebuttal" won't work if Marie is across the room from Frank. It works best if Frank is next to Marie and she can give him a look. Right?

Clarity. At any point along the way, the clarity can be muddled, and then the joke, or even the point of your story, is muddled. The shot has to be framed correctly so that we can see Marie next to Frank as he says this line. Then in the editing, if you don't stay on that shot for the correct amount of time, or you don't cut to it at the right moment before the line, the clarity could be lost.

Usually when we're on the floor during the show, I'll say, "Use that take" to the editor. And Pat Barnett, our editor for all nine years, is taking notes. We have a room in our office building that's an editing suite with the Macintosh computers and the Final Cut Pro, and all the Avid equipment and I'm Jewish so I don't know how to work it. But Pat does, and a few days later, when she's gotten the film back and it's been made into something digital, instead of going through reels of film like in olden times, it's all in the computer on the hard drive. And you can call up anything at any moment. And by anything, it's what all four cameras were shooting at any given moment during every take of every episode.

So we have all that. And from that Pat makes a rough assemblage for me. I go upstairs to the editing room and I start at the beginning of the episode. Right away, if the first moment feels wrong to me, we stop and examine all the possibilities. Let's cut it, show me another angle of that, show me all four angles. What was Robert doing while Marie was saying that? "Give me the B camera for this line, then go to C, then go to X, and back to A, then back to B." That's how you put together a show—making the moments clearer and clearer with each one of these choices.

You make it clear by taking out the extraneous, which hones the focus. You know how long to stay on a shot to maybe get an even richer laugh out of it because the look on an actor's face in close-up is so hilarious that you want to stay there. Don't cut away so fast after this joke; let it land. Ray could say something funny, and if we cut away too fast, it doesn't land, it doesn't have a second. Sometimes the actor's face is great right after the line, and because of that, it seems to come from a real person. They really say it, there is some thought behind the line, and the scene is not just joke, joke, joke, joke. It's talking, and it's coming from people. This makes all the difference. And it should go by you, the audience, seamlessly, because you're involved in the story.

The emphasis on a single syllable can make or break the line, too. The wrong emphasis kills the whole thing. Remember *Second City TV*? There was a sketch with John Candy and Eugene Levy—they were the Polish polka-playing Shmenge brothers, and they'd introduce themselves: "Hi, I'm Yosh Shmengee," one of them would say. And the other would say, "And I'm Stan *Shmengee.*" He'd put the emphasis on the "Shmenge," when most people who have that last name would put the emphasis on the first name. And so the phrase "He just shmengee'd that line" was born. We use it whenever the wrong emphasis is screwing up the clarity of a line. And sometimes, that's all that's wrong with a scene. When I'm talking with the actors, sometimes the direction is "Hit this word like this." And there are some actors who do not like taking this kind of direction. They might feel that deciding how to read the lines is their job. And for you to tell them how to do it takes their soul away. I always thought they could look at it another way, and our cast did. Here is the result we want. We trust you enough as an artist to fill in your inner life and make that your own as long as we get to this result. Smile at the end of this line. It's up to you then to figure out: How do I do that organically, naturally, so that the motivation looks genuine? So you're getting simple direction. You're getting what we need to see. Yes, we have conversations about what we're thinking and what we're meaning, and why this and why that and why not. But at the end of the day, hit this word. It'll be clearer and, then, funnier. And don't shmengee.

It's all a struggle toward simplicity and clarity—from the writers' story, to the show in front of the live audience, to the show as broadcast on television.

Sometimes it's very apparent in The Writers' Room: Oh, that's obviously a great show to do. And sometimes it's a goddamn struggle to figure out what an episode is about. What is it about? That's at the bottom of everything. What is it about? What is this scene about? What is this line about? What is this word about? Or, is it worth stopping the scene for that joke? What if it doesn't advance the story—and not every line has to advance the story—we *are* in the comedy business—but is it worth stopping for Frank to insult his wife at this moment? Usually, you bet it is. Everyone has his or her part to play. Everyone has his or her character that we look forward to seeing. We sit there watching; like you, we look forward to Robert being jealous of Raymond. We look forward to maybe Robert trumping Raymond or then getting slammed again. We look forward to Ray getting caught by Debra. We look forward to Debra being slammed by Marie. But as the story is being written, those are not the conscious thoughts. The conscious thought is the story. What is the story? What is it about? Those other things we'll fill in naturally. Yes, we understand because we know the characters—that Frank will react this way and Marie will react that way. But as the years go on, you start to want to shake it up. Well, what if today they didn't react that way? What if today Debra said, "That's great, Ray. Good for you." Maybe that could happen someday. What would that do? No one is one-dimensional. We're trying to make multidimensional characters that seem like real people. What does Frank love about Marie? That's a good question. And don't say food.

Sometimes the comedy comes from overturning the expectations. I'll always say, "What if we did the opposite?" Part of my job as showrunner is to be the devil's advocate for everybody else. And

I expect them to do it with me (and they do; it's annoying). If we didn't keep that up, we'd get tired, and you'd get bored. There'd be no surprise. It's just good storytelling to shake it up once in a while—Debra's the one who's wrong about the canister. Now, if it's working, you don't need to do the opposite, or take a look at it from another point of view. If it works, great. But if it's lying there, if it's just fine but it's not singing, what's the problem? What's preventing this from being the best show ever done anywhere? Maybe too big a question. Okay, what is this scene missing? Occasionally it's missing high stakes, in other words, as close to a life-and-death situation as possible, and that could happen over a can opener. Occasionally it's missing something we haven't seen before, a surprise, and the surprise can sometimes be that Debra is not attacking Ray, Ray is attacking Debra. He goes on the offensive; he's never done that before. So we've got to justify his doing that. You have to justify every action and attitude the character takes, or they don't make sense. If your script is staying in the real world, if you're writing something outrageous that's expected to be believed as something that could happen, you've got to justify the outrageous behavior. How can someone drive a car through a house? The crazy thing that happens in this scene must be justified. You've got to earn it. You can't just say, "Well, it happens because it's funny," because then you stink and it stinks and you've added stink to the world. Justify getting there.

How does Ray burn the kitchen down? We worked very hard on justifying that very thing in Mike Royce's episode "Tissues." It all started with Mike, who came in to work complaining that he never gets to make decisions in his house, and we all chimed in, the wife rules everything, the wife does everything, we hate wives. So we thought that if we did this story, Ray should be in charge of a little thing. Give him a little thing like a tissue; I bought some tissues, and my wife bothered me. So Ray gets tissues. What happens if he suddenly is allowed to make that little bitty decision? Well, I think he has to burn the house down. So then we work backward from there to justify it.

In the first act of the show, Debra and Ray are having an ant problem in the kitchen, and, against Ray's wishes, Debra decides they should take the kids out for dinner. It's a disaster, and when they get home, Ray turns to his wife and says, "Well, did you get what you wanted?" This stupid and dangerous thing to say to an already angry wife turns into a fight about how Ray feels he never has any say in his own life. He goes on the offensive. Debra says, "The reason you're not allowed to make decisions around the house is because you always make bad decisions. It's like that hose you bought, this two-foot hose that doesn't even reach the flowers." He says, "It's a perfectly good hose. You put your thumb over the end, and it sprays farther. That's what people do." Debra says, "Well, you don't get to decide things in the house because you don't lift a finger to help around here. When do you ever do the laundry or wash the dishes?" Ray says, "Maybe I would wash a dish if I didn't have to look at those disgusting curtains hanging over the sink, which I had no say in choosing."

Now, after a bit more marriage war, Ray actually makes a rational argument for his own brainpower. And it's agreed that Ray is going to be allowed to make some decisions in the house. So he goes to the store and comes back with a lot of stuff that he thinks is great—fabulous bargains. He found some tissues on sale and he brings home grocery bags full of a dozen boxes of them. Not only that but, since he's making household decisions now, he got some notebooks. He got some paper kites for the children to play with. He got this organic ant spray; he sprays the counter with it. (From the first line of the show, "Ray, there's ants all over the sink," we've established the ant problem, and we keep that alive through the episode.) But the tissues are what the family stops on. "We like the tissues that Debra buys." Ray's brand is cheap, they're only a hundred count, and Robert makes fun of them. You screwed up, Ray; you can't even buy tissues, and they all leave.

And so now Ray's pissed, because he can't even buy freakin' tissues, right? And he hates that Debra, especially, will never let him make any damn decisions in the house. He doesn't need this crap, and he's at least going to make his own dinner. Well, all the stuff is laid out on the counter, he's had a tissue in his hand and he slams it down, and he's going to make himself a can of soup. He opens the soup and turns on the burner; then the phone rings, and he gets the phone. He's talking to Gianni about golf and he's bitching about what it's like to live there, and behind him the burner from the stove is too close to the tissue that he's just put down, and it lights on fire. And then the ant spray that he's got all over the countertop acts as a propellant. The fire follows the trail of ant spray to the notebooks, the paper kites, leading to the big bag of tissues. . . . The curtains, which he has complained about earlier, are now on fire. He hangs up the phone, and sees it.

Raymond freaks out—he takes a can of soda from the table and shakes it on the flames. It doesn't do anything. He's panicking; he doesn't know what to do. He runs out the front door. He then comes running back in with the hose and he gets about as far as the couch and he gets yanked back—a callback to a joke that's been set up. One of the best laughs we've ever had on the show was that moment, because the setup had been forgotten. And when it was remembered again, it was remembered at the exact moment that Ray remembers.

The house is on fire. So what he does is he tries spraying from the couch, and then he unscrews the sprayer and puts his thumb over it and he tries, and it reaches maybe to the other side of the couch. And Debra comes downstairs. "What's going on!?" And he turns on her. "The house is on fire!" Spraying her with the hose. "It's on fire, it's on fire!" Debra screams, seeing her kitchen on fire, and she runs over. Right under the stove is a fire extinguisher, and she opens it and she sprays and she puts out the fire. The audience was screaming, clapping for Debra—laughing at how easily the wife does it, how powerful the wife is. Where's the husband? He's still in the living room, his little hose dribbling.

Insanity, yes. But justified. It *could* happen.

While we were talking about the technical part of actually burning our kitchen set, we figured out it's funniest if it happens when he doesn't notice it, even if he's in the room. The audience sees it, but he doesn't. And when he discovers it, that could be funny, too. And then we need a physical bit that is funny on top of that. In other words, he could just scream and run out of the house, but what if he tried to put it out? And we say, "What if he had a short hose?" And we instantly think, we've got to plant that earlier. And that information about the hose was hidden in a list of other things, like he wanted a couch that had three footrests. It's good writing if the setup is funny in and of itself. Then the audience doesn't know they're being set up—that's a good setup. It's not dry, it's not boring, it's not what we call "pipey"—as in, it's so obviously information that the audience needs to know just to understand what the hell is going on, it's as if we're laying pipe. We don't want the audience to know it's just exposition, the part they have to sit through before we get to the kitchen burning down.

The viewers are very savvy and watch a lot of television. They understand the form of the sitcom, even if they can't articulate it; they inherently, subconsciously, unconsciously know it, so you play with that. You mislead them into thinking that this is just a little episode about tissues and there are discussions from the characters that they expect, that have a deeper meaning (it's never just about the tissues), and you hope that they don't see this big stunt coming.

When the kitchen starts to go on fire, not only is the audience surprised, the viewers now have a sense of intimacy and involvement—they care about the story and the characters. The best is when there's a thematic element going on, too—the wife is going to come down, she knows where the fire extinguisher is, she's going to put it out one, two, three, and we're going to cut to Ray with his emasculated hose. And the thematic element is, This is the reason you don't make the decisions. This is the reason. The wife is better. That's what we're saying.

By the way, there was a discussion about how many blasts of the fire extinguisher Debra should do. Three. I don't know any other way to describe it; it just seems like three is usually the best way, rhythmically, because everything is music. And it's short blast, short blast, long blast. So the first blast is like a surprise to Debra (she probably never had to use the extinguisher before), the second establishes that the thing works, and the last one is the song. The first two are warm-ups, and then the song. If it were a machine gun, it would be short burst, short burst, long burst. Because you're hoping for a giant release from the audience. The fire is out, and Debra did it. And it comes, triumphantly, at the end of a long note of music.

Then she turns slowly . . . and she looks at him, and he's there with his hose. And it's still running water into the living room, because he's in shock.

We had ten different lines for Ray, most of which you can't say on TV, but we still did them anyway for our gag reel, and to make the studio audience laugh. The water is coming out, and the laugh, and then what's he finally going to say to top it? "I have to go to the bathroom" was a favorite. The one we wound up using was, "Got rid of the ants." He did something good. See? You thought I just burned down the kitchen.

At the top of the episode we set up Ray complaining about the curtains. He hates those curtains. So it's nice that he's burned the curtains down. And so, in the tag, we open with Ray at the end of the table, Debra at the middle of the table, and a man on the other side of the table, showing some fabric. "The damage isn't that extensive. I have some wallpaper samples in the car, but here are some curtains samples, if you want to look." As Debra starts thumbing through them, Ray pulls his chair around to look over her shoulder. And she just looks at him. He slides his chair back to where he was sitting. The end. Say it without saying it is a great rule. You don't want to be so on the nose; you want the subtext to come through. First of all, you have to have text before there can be subtext, right? But the show, what is it about? You don't want to say it blatantly in lines; you want it to be there, understood. You never want to say "I am angry." That's bad writing, right? Too on the nose. So you want to say it without saying it. You want to say I love you without saying it.

The first episode after the pilot in 1996 was the "I Love You" episode. Ray doesn't say I love you. He has trouble with it. He always finds that it sounds phony when he says it. To him, it sounds like he's in a bad movie. "It doesn't sound real coming out of my mouth." (Ray's problem *and* the writers' problem.) And Debra wants desperately for him to say it, and they have a fight about it. He's going to go away on a business trip, and this is no way to leave. We see him in the bedroom packing. He starts to go and he looks back at the bed, and it's not made. He makes the bed and he does a bad job of it. He's not good at making the bed, but he tries very hard. He bends all the way over the bed to try to tuck in the sheet on the other side and he tosses his pillow on his side, but her pillow he stops to fluff up a little bit. He takes some time with it, places it on her side, and then smoothes it out with his hand.

And she sees him. He has said it without saying it. And she's just kind of looking at him, and he says, "I'm sorry." She goes up to him. "It's fine. You don't have to say it. I get it." And they kiss, and Ray says, "I love you." And she cracks up laughing. And he goes, "I knew it! I knew it! See? I can't say it! See? No more! No more! That's it, from now on, you get only cards from me."

If we want the audience to care about the show, we have to care about it, and we worry and fret over every detail. I have to save for another book the decisions about costume, hair, and set design; personal dramas; how the show is advertised; how the film is developed—there's a tremendous amount of work that goes into making a half hour look seamless. Fred Astaire would practice dancing until his feet were bleeding. Every move, everything, where to turn, every decision, how to hold his head, his hands, every split second of that dance had been choreographed to within an inch of its life so that when you watch it, it appears effortless. Same with this. Same with any good play, film, TV show, book, painting, vagina sculpture.

You shouldn't think to look under the socks; you just enjoy the dancing.

11

A Couple of Weeks

President Clinton's last year in office was 2000. I had been writing jokes for him for eight years, and he was now leaving. I blamed the jokes. This had been a good gig. A high school friend of my brother's, Mark Katz, was Clinton's go-to guy whenever humor season descended on Washington. (No, it's not year-round; there's actually a season: April, when the Gridiron Dinner, the Radio and TV Correspondents' Dinner, and the big one, the White House Correspondents' Dinner, each call on the president to make a funny speech.) Mark had always brought me in to help, and it was an unbelievable honor to have lines I worked on spoken by our leader.

The dinners had gone well, thanks to Clinton's marvelous delivery, and Mark and I had always talked about making a short video with the president that could play at the Correspondents' Dinner, but the president never had the time. That last year, however, he did have some spare moments, and we decided that that is what our little movie would be about: the president having nothing to do now that his eight years are almost up, and so he pads around the White House trying to keep himself busy. He washes the car, mows the lawn, answers the phones, does origami. I wrote it with Mark and Jeff Shesol, one of President Clinton's brilliant speechwriters, and to our amazement, the president read it and was on board.

I flew to Washington to direct the video, all the while wondering, *What world am I in?* It's one thing to tell Raymond to spill sauce on himself but this was absolutely unbelievable. . . . I was going to have to forget that this was the president in order to stop the nausea.

The White House Correspondents' Dinner was going to be Saturday night, and I arrived at the White House the Sunday before. We were told we would have three hours with the president, and I thought, *Well, that's a good chunk of time, but not in the movie world. How can we get everything?* We did as much anticipatory work as we could—this was a low-budget film, because the Clinton administration did not spend much on such things. I had three cameramen ready (one was my brother, Richard, on his home Handycam), and we figured out where we would place them for each scene. We scoped out the different locations—the press briefing room, the Old Executive Office Building, the Rose Garden, the Oval Office, the screening room. For some reason, we would not be allowed to film in the White House kitchen. We couldn't get clearance, even from the chief of staff. Why? Were we afraid the Russians were going to learn our baking secrets? Never got an answer why. It's still a great mystery, but we adapted. After some tough negotiations, we got the laundry room. When we were ready to shoot, we were suddenly told we'd have a half hour Tuesday afternoon, and that was all we could have with the president. Okay, I know he's the president, but . . . what the hell? It's impossible, I thought, but I had to take what I could get. Maybe I'd start, and the White House folks would see that it takes a bit longer to film something than it does to watch it. But there was no way we could get our five-minute video shot in a half hour.

President Clinton arrived at our first location, the briefing room, for our first scene. He is very tall, handsome, and charming.

And there are few more brilliant people on the planet. He was happy and ready to go.

Joining us for this scene, where the president decides to make the most of his final days in office, was General Hugh Shelton, chairman of the Joint Chiefs of Staff, in uniform. The scene called for our president to sit across from the general and play Battleship. President Clinton loved the idea of playing a game in the briefing room with the general, but he was unfamiliar with Battleship. So among the honors I've had in my life, I got to teach the president the game. As I was doing so, General Shelton said proudly, "You know, I've got the electronic version." I said, "Sir, you've got the real version."

The scene went well. It would occupy about ten seconds of screen time and took up half our allotted shoot time. I knew that we would have to move faster, even if it meant running the president of the United States around the White House like a monkey in a Vegas act. But the president enjoyed himself, and said we could have another half hour that night with him. We were getting some good stuff. A lot was one take, not just because we had to, but because he was good. Very good. Almost a scarily good actor.

We were doing a scene in the Oval Office, the president sitting at his desk, and about forty staff people were standing around, watching the filming. One of the highlights of my life was just as we were about to start taping, looking across the Oval Office of the White House, and catching my brother's eye. You could tell we were both thinking the same thing: *Why would the government allow two little kids in here?*

A minute later, we got to a part in the script where President Clinton would say, "Yahtzee!" (as in the game). And the president says, "Yahzee!" No T. "That's okay," I say (maybe he never had any games), and we take it again.

"Yahzee."

I say, "Sir, it's '*Yaht*-zee.'" He looks at me blankly. I repeat, "Yahtzee. *Yaaaht*-zee."

And he says, "That's what I said."

I think most people would have left it alone at this point. Most smart people. I, however, continue. "I'm not hearing the T, sir. *Yaht*-zee." The president says (with a slight touch of annoyance now), "I thought I was doing that. Yahzee."

I say, "*Yaht*zee. It's Y-a-—" He cuts me off. "I know. Y-a-t-z-e."

There's a moment as the staff looks down at their shoes and the carpeting. I think for a second and then say, "Perfect."

One more take, and . . . it's close enough. We wrapped the scene, and my brother rushed over to me and took me aside. He was mortified. He said, "Your tone of voice when correcting the president of the United States was the same as when you correct me while calling me a dick."

"But he has to pronounce the word right—how would he look?" I did it for him—for the country.

My brother was right. *I'm an idiot,* I thought, *I've blown the whole thing.* But President Clinton was more than gracious, he knew that we were just working and we actually got along very well, chatting through the White House en route to our various locations. When we were done for the night, we were told he wanted to finish the movie in one more half-hour session on Saturday. That was great, but Saturday was the day of the event. We'd have to shoot in the morning, edit the tape that afternoon, and rush over just in time for the event to show it.

I had been asking for Mrs. Clinton's involvement since the beginning, but was told by staff members, "Hillary is not going to know about the video. If she hears about it, and doesn't like the idea, she'll tell Bill, and it's over." Well, after we started, it seems Mrs. Clinton's husband told her himself about all these scenes he was getting to do. First thing next morning, "Hillary wants to be in the video." We're told she'd do anything. She was very nice. We had a scene where the first lady is in the backseat of her limo, and she tells the camera, "I'm sure Bill has everything under control," then shuts the door and speeds off. A Secret Service agent wouldn't let us do that. He insisted that it's his job to open and close the car door for her—which would slow down and blow the bit. I convinced him to open the door for her and shut it partially, then get in the car and let us do the shot. It was a tough decision for this gentleman to compromise, but I guess everybody has insecurities about his job.

The Clintons watched each other's scenes. I've never seen anyone laugh so hard as the president did when I got to tell him that when the limo took off, he'd run out of the back of the White House with a brown paper bag, yelling, "Honey, wait! Wait! You forgot your lunch!" We'd then see, through the rear window of the limo as it sped away, the president get smaller and smaller, holding the bag.

In the next scene, the president, because he's got so much free time, rides a bicycle through the massive halls of the Old Executive Office Building. A couple of senior staff members thought it would be a great idea if Terry McAuliffe, the president's friend, joined him for a bike ride through the halls. Not only that, but they thought it'd be great if the president sat on Mr. McAuliffe's handlebars while McAuliffe pedaled. Now, I always welcome input, but the creative juices were flowing maybe a little too freely that day through our nation's capital. I had to speak up. I said, "First of all, I can't be responsible for the leader of the free world's breaking his neck. Second, wouldn't we be saying with that shot that President Clinton is Terry McAuliffe's girlfriend?" Did they want "Raindrops Keep Falling on My Head" in the background?

Cooler heads prevailed. We got all our footage and zoomed to editing. Now, of course, the president had to approve the video before it was shown to the world that night. There was a meeting right before the event in the Map Room, where wars are planned. It's where they rehearse the speech and everybody has to be in their tuxes already because they're going right out the back door of that room into the presidential motorcade to the dinner. The people who run the country are in that room. And the president is asking for the tape. We're getting calls in the edit bay: "Where's the tape?" And we're late because we're editing in Arlington on the same day we shot it and the same night we're showing it, and the computer actually broke down for two hours. We finally finished, and my brother and I jumped in a cab, sped across town, ran into the White House with the tape, and we're stopped by Secret Service. "You can't go in there."

"But the president wants this tape!" I say, sounding like a very bad actor in a cable movie.

They won't let us in the room because we're not in our tuxedos, and there is no time to change afterward—we have to go right into the motorcade with them after the meeting. My brother and I get pointed to a small White House bathroom to change into our tuxedos. Together. We're cramped and frantic. The Secret Service men could hear lines like this coming from inside that bathroom: "Help me with my cummerbund!" and "Those are my pants, you idiot!" We're cursing and sweating, and knowing President Clinton is probably getting angry, and we're futzing around with cufflinks and loose tuxedo buttons in the wrong holes. And I finally dress, wipe the sweat off my head, and enter the room—here's the tape.

My friend Mark, who got me into this, says, "You stand over here." He pushes me to stand next to the president. "You made it, you stand there."

So the president's standing in front of a TV and a VCR, and I'm right next to him. Everyone gathers around. They put it on, and it starts, and for approximately the first twenty seconds, no reaction. No laughs at all. Nothing. I'm just thinking, *Ohhhhhh, I've ruined the country. I've humiliated the president. I have to move to Poland.* And then Mr. President gives a little chuckle, and when he does, it's okay for the rest of us to chuckle, and then a little more, and then President Clinton is slapping his leg like he's in Arkansas and actually guffawing. Then he's hugging me at the end, and Mrs. Clinton gives me a kiss, and we zoom in to the motorcade and to the event, and they put it on for the two thousand people in the room and for C-SPAN. The tape was still wet. It went on, and then my life changed. The reaction was huge. And it was all because of President Clinton's performance. He was hilarious. It was something no one had really seen before, a president still in office giving a screen performance, being *intentionally* funny (if you want to see it, type this into your computer very carefully—otherwise you get porn or soda exploding: http://politicalhumor.about.com/library/blclintonfinaldaysvideo.htm). The *Today* show led with the tape the next morning. I was invited on a bunch of shows, and then something really big happened. A friend of mine, Tony DeSena, calls up and says, "Somebody wants to have lunch with you." This person saw the tape and wanted a copy of it. And Tony said to him, "I know the guy who made it. You can have lunch with him if you want." Who wanted the tape? Johnny Carson.

So I had lunch with Johnny Carson. I brought Ray with me, and we had two hours with him. I have to say, for me, that was maybe even more exciting than the president thing. Because if you think about it, there've been several presidents.

Mr. Carson was fantastic to us. He had been retired for eight years, had no intention of coming back, and had many great stories he very generously shared. Best advice from him concerned entertainers who use their platform for other than entertaining. He said, "Just do your act and get the hell off the stage."

So I thank President Clinton for opening these doors for me. Whenever I see him, even years later now (he remembers everything and everybody), he says, "Phil! The man who made me famous." The week I spent working in the White House was truly surreal. When I got home from that trip to Washington, I said to my wife, "You know, if you tell the most powerful man what to do, and he *does* it, doesn't that make *you* the most powerful man in the world?"

My wife said, "Pick up your socks."

The following month, May 2000, I was in New York, working with another president, my friend Leslie Moonves, on his annual upfronts. Since *Raymond* had been on the air, I had helped Les with his speech every year. I knew we would never have even gotten on television, let alone stayed there, without Les's support and so I was always happy to pitch in and always flattered that he'd ask me. It's a big production, and I help with jokes in the speech, the clarity of the presentation, visual bits, and with Les's delivery. He's another natural, by the way. He used to be an actor, and this creative side of him is what I believe makes him the best at what he does. He's not just business, he *has* a creative side.

While humor season is going on in Washington, pilot season is happening in Los Angeles. Each network commissions about a hundred and twenty scripts a year. Out of those, maybe twenty-five pilots get made. Out of those, maybe ten shows get on the air, and that includes all the dramas, comedies, and reality shows. Almost all the pilots get made in April, they're sent to the networks at the end of the month, and then the networks scramble in a mad race to assemble the fall schedule for presentation in New York the second week of May. This allows them about a week or less to make the decisions that will affect the rest of their broadcast year, and that determine what we all have to watch on TV. I wouldn't say that this methodology contributes to everything stinking, but if you said it, I might not shake my head to deny it. Now, because I worked closely with Les, and probably because *Raymond* was successful, he would sometimes ask me to give notes on the cut-downs, the collections of five-minute clips from each pilot for inclusion in the upfront show. I would give notes as an outsider, an audience member, mostly asking questions to determine if the cut-down was as clear as it could be, or if a bit could be made funnier in editing. But then there were times when I would be asked my opinion of the actual show.

This was a tough spot. But I was asked for an opinion, and I eventually understood that it would be taken as just another opinion, of which there are many at any place of business. Truth be told, I didn't like this at all. What if they listened to me? Jobs were on the line—every show employs about a hundred and fifty people. I could throw up just thinking about this. Who was I to decide anyone's fate? I fell asleep on the bed at the museum.

On a particular night in May, the night before the 2000 CBS upfronts at Carnegie Hall, Les had his senior staff assembled around a large table in a conference room upstairs at Black Rock, the CBS headquarters on Sixth Avenue. It was dark. The lights were off everywhere else in the building except in the conference room high up on one of the top floors. The group seated around the long conference table included the heads of marketing, promotion, research, drama and comedy development, and scheduling. The guys had big folders of information in front of them. Contracts and big piles of computer research and the phone numbers of hit men. I was in there, too. All the other fellas were wearing ties over their long-sleeve tailored shirts. I had on a short-sleeve polo and a face that said, "Let me outta here."

We were going over the speech. Les was reading it aloud, and we'd stop for fixes and suggestions. He came to an introduction of a show and stopped midway through the paragraph. "I don't know if I can present this thing at Carnegie Hall tomorrow," he said. "How am I gonna look presenting this?"

There was some discussion of the show's merits, and then Les asked, "Phil, did you see this cut-down?"

"Me?"

Everyone else looked at me as if I had just passed gas at Westminster Abbey. They were not crazy about the fact that I was even in their top-secret meeting, let alone asked something by The Boss. I told Les that I had not seen this cut-down. As some in the room protested, Les found the tape and put it on. I watched it. It was clearly terrible. It was such a stupid show I was actually surprised when it was over because Les turned to me with a straight face and asked, "What do you think?"

The room turned to ice. It was late. I was hungry. A smarter guy would not have said anything in that position, or maybe smiled and said, "Very nice." But I didn't like the show. I couldn't believe it even got made. And so I shrugged and I softly said something like, "Isn't it enough with this kind of thing already?"

This comment did not go over well with the other people in the room—some of whom had championed this very show—and they justifiably resented my answer.

"I don't think Phil should—I don't think that's right to say and—I don't think we should be asking his opinion—This is not his—"

And Les says, "No, no, I wanted to know. I asked him and I wanted an outside opinion, that's all. I'm allowed."

There was some more discussion about the merits of this program and more about how it was completely out of line for me to give my opinion about a show. "Why is he even here?"

Sometimes it's fun to be fought over, like at a dinner party, when ladies surround you, vying for their turn to ask what Hollywood is really like. This was not one of those times. (And the dinner-party thing has never happened to me.) My polo shirt now had those giant rings of sweat under the arms. Les then asked the head of research how this show had tested. The head of research pulled out a huge sheet of paper, looked it over, and said, "Tested very well." *Unbelievable,* I thought to myself. This is how civilization ends. Everything is tested to death, under unrealistic conditions, and testing's main use has become ass covering. So that any given executive doesn't have to take the blame for a decision but can point to the numbers when the thing tanks, and say, "It wasn't my decision; it tested well." If every show tests well that the networks put on, there's clearly something wrong—for instance, the only reason the Stupid Show tested "very well" is because the audience recognized the lead. The quality of the show meant nothing. "I know that guy! I turn the knob on my approval meter to the right." End of testing. And so the show goes on and it stinks because that's not how anybody watches television, but sometimes enough people watch to justify the process, and then the end of civilization.

Les rubbed his chin, clearly in a quandary. Then he said, "Where's that show that I liked?" and as most of the room tried to dissuade Les from looking for a last-minute replacement for the Stupid Show, Les rummaged around the floor in a pile of discarded tapes, saying, "I just want Phil to see this thing." He found the tape he was looking for and put it in the VCR.

Oh God, I thought to myself. *This'll stink, too, and he just said he likes it.* And the tape starts, and it's like a cop show, but it's kind of cool. There's cool music and there are cool effects and it's shot very well. And they're finding out stuff in an interesting way. And I thought, *That's kind of cool.*

Then it ends, and Les turns to me and asks, "What do you think of that?"

"Now that, I would watch."

"Why?"

"Because it's cool. I like seeing how they figure it out, and it's clever the way they find this and that."

Les says to Head of Research, "How did it test?" Head of Research opens his giant stack of papers and he looks and he looks . . . he says, "A little less than the other show."

Les rubs his chin again and goes, "Hmmm," as in "What do I do?" And I guess because I was so far into this now that there was no turning back, and because everyone hated me anyway, and because I had started to care, and because I was hungry, and because it was now crucial to the future of the world that Les Moonves, a man trapped in the machine, pick the show that *he liked,* I lost my mind.

"Les! You just told me that's the one that you like!"

"I know, but . . ."

I leaned across the table. “Well, okay, but, so it tested a little less. I mean, no offense”—I turned to Mr. Research—“but did we ever test the testing? Every show that gets on tests well, and 99.9 percent of them crap out after two episodes!”

I had clearly gone off the deep end. I continued to Les, “Come on! You’re allowed to pick *one show* that you like and put it on! It’s all a crap shoot, anyway, so you may as well, right? You just said you like this one, right?”

He goes, “Yeah. I don’t know. I don’t know.” And we moved on. Nothing else was said about it for the rest of that night. I left the building just hoping Les would do what he wanted, forget the numbers side, remember why he got in the business in the first place, maybe talk to the kid in himself who wanted to be in the high school play. If nothing else, it would mean that there were still people at the controls.

I have no idea what happened that night after I went home. But the next day, *CSI* was on the schedule.

12

Family

I'll tell you the craziest we ever got on the show: Robert thinks that the girl he's brought home could be "The One" and Ray sees her in a private moment. She catches a fly at the dinner table and eats it. Only Ray sees this, and he stands in shock for several moments as the scene continues around him. Finally, he is compelled to tell his brother, "She's not the one." Robert doesn't believe Ray when Ray tells him what he's witnessed, and after getting mad at Ray for being jealous of his happiness, Robert goes to the girl's apartment. Once there, it looks like it's going to be a romantic evening . . . she's going to step into the washroom for a moment and meet Robert in the bedroom. Robert goes into the bedroom and hears something odd. He turns on the light, revealing that the room is filled with aquariums, frogs in every one. He notices that the whole room has a frog motif, with paintings, and stuffed plushy frogs, and plenty of live, ribbeting frogs. Robert begins to realize that Ray may have been telling the truth. He panics. He doesn't know what to do, so he starts to go out the window. Our frog lady now enters and catches him in mid-window. Robert explains, . . . "Good-bye." And drops out of sight.

Sounds fanciful, yes? What happened to the "Could this happen?" rule? This could never happen, right?

It happened. It happened to Ray's brother, and it was worse than what we did on the show. In real life, they weren't frogs, they were snakes.

Ray's brother picked up a girl in a bar, went back to her apartment, and the room was filled with snakes. Then he went into her bathroom because he was freaking out. The bathroom was filled with occult and witchcraft stuff, and so he went out the window. And he's a *policeman.* That's how scared he was. So we heard about that, and working backward from that story, we asked: What would be the inciting incident? Ray came up with "What if I see her eat a fly?" Then we filled her room with frogs to tie that in. Insane, but you know what? People have done stranger things. It's about as out there as we've ever been, but there *are* crazy people around. This was a crazy lady. They exist. Do we do that every week? No. But still, even in this episode, there was a dramatic hook. We had a reason for the craziness. Robert comes back to Ray's house, and it has to be that crazy a story because it's important that his mother doesn't believe him. His mother thinks he's making all kinds of excuses because he's gay.

What makes it funny, we hope, is that what happened to Robert certainly sounds crazy, and yet we all saw it. We saw the girl eat a fly and we saw Robert go into the apartment with the frogs. He's not making it up. But to a mother who can't understand why her forty-something son isn't married and maybe doubts his sexuality, this is . . . "Just admit it already. It's okay! 'Hello, I'm queer and now I'm here!' " Marie tearfully yells at Robert, "Just find somebody, anybody. I don't care. You're ripping my heart out. For God's sake, do you want to die alone?" And Frank says, "Yes!" And then, "Oh, him." But for the most part, this scene is drama. Robert says, "Ma, enough. I'm forty-four years old and I haven't found my other half.

Maybe it's time to just accept the fact that there might not be another half . . . for this." And he points to himself. Then he gets up and leaves. It's the first time ever in seven years that we didn't cut this moment with a joke. We always feel it's our job to make the audience laugh, but we had something else to do so we left the second act without a laugh. Frank stands up and says, "Wait, son." (We never heard "son" from Frank either.) And they all are just standing there as Robert goes out alone—fade out.

After commercial, we go to the bar where Robert's having a drink because he's so depressed. He sits at the bar, takes a scotch, and sips. A waiter comes by with a tray full of drinks and trips over his giant feet, goes flying out of frame, and we hear a huge crash. Robert, shocked and embarrassed, stands up and we see that the drinks have all fallen over on somebody and they're cleaning up this person. It's a girl, and she turns, and it's Amy.

That's how we reintroduced her. They had broken up and gotten back together many times, but several months had passed since we'd seen her. She looks up . . . and the audience reacted. . . . We left this in the soundtrack: You can hear a woman in the audience gasp, "Amy!" On Robert's face you see he's about to say, "Amy," and we cut.

In The Room this episode was discussed at the end of the previous season. We were planning season seven and we started with this question: How do we end the series? Again, I honestly never saw how the show could go past seven years. What the hell would we write about? So what's a good ending for this family? Ray and Debra move away? Who would really enjoy that? Frank and/or Marie dies? *There's* some fun for the people. No, the only character whose situation in life can improve dramatically is Robert. How can we change Robert's life? The Room starts throwing ideas around: Should he finally get married to Amy? We should get him married. We could have an arc of stories revolving around Robert's engagement and wedding. That was really the impetus. So, first story in this arc: Let's give Robert one more horrible date. He's had a series of them over the years. We can't do any more dating shows with him, anyway. After seven years, enough already. We talk in The Room about bad date stories. Tom Caltabiano only has great date stories, so he's no help at all. Ray tells us about his brother and this thing with the snakes, and it went from there.

We'd then do an episode about Robert asking for Amy's hand in marriage, "Just a Formality," with the introduction of Amy's family. It's a pretty big risk to marry off a regular character. A potential "jump the shark" moment, TV-show slang for the moment when the staff has run out of ideas and are grasping for anything to breathe life into the show. It comes from late in the run on *Happy Days* when they put Fonzie on water skis and had him literally jump over a shark. It's all downhill once the shark has been jumped. In other words, the audience could feel that the story would change too much of what the show is for them. In this case, the dynamic of Robert being the outsider. If we then marry him and introduce another family, some in the audience could say that the series didn't exist anymore the way they wanted it to. That's a valid thing to say. However, we had no choice. We did not want to jump a shark, but the characters have to keep growing or the show gets stale. This growth can come in revelations of character through actions they take or events that happen to them.

For example, Robert got engaged and even Brad Garrett thought, *Oh no, this is the end of my character.* Because he'd been a loser. He'd been the odd man out. If he gets married, he's afraid that's all gone. Now he's a winner. My attitude was, it all just gets richer. Robert marries Amy, and at first he thinks he has what he thinks Raymond has. However, once he gets married he will see he's still Robert. He still doesn't have the place in his mother's heart that Raymond has, and so he may feel worse. Robert could have everything Raymond has—he could even have twin boys. He could have triplets. He could have a better life in every way than Raymond has, but he will never be Raymond. The circumstances may change, but not his character. We're changing the sit, not the com. Brad generously went along with this, and I gave him a cookie.

I want every episode to have some truth revealed so that it's something that the audience identifies with in their lives, that has resonance. That's the whole point. And if you work in the sitcom form, which is fast, like a short story, the challenge is: How do you get that emotional punch or meaning in that short form? It helps to have great actors, like our regular cast, and then we got more help from Georgia Engel, Fred Willard, and Chris Elliott, who joined us as Amy's family.

And what about Amy? That actress, Monica Horan. Elevating her recurring role could feel a bit like cronyism, no? Someone even said to me, "You just want her to marry Robert because she's your wife." I'd love to take credit for Monica's being on the show, but it wasn't me—it was the guys in The Room. Yes, I approved it. I even knew how to get in touch with her. But I would never have foisted my wife on America. What if she was unwelcome? It would only make more trouble for me at home. And I had enough. But I have to say, after fifteen years of marriage and four years of sinful living before that, I still like her. For those of you who don't know Monica Horan, yes, Debra is somewhat based on her, but I would argue that Debra is an Everywife, or at least every wife who's had to put up with a schlemiel for a husband. The character of Amy is really who my wife is, and beyond that, she's an impossibly decent, cheerful, optimistic, selfless person. She's so friendly, just like Amy, it really does take her an hour to leave a party because when it's time to go, she embarks on her good-bye tour. She volunteers her time to all kinds of causes and truly thinks the best of people. We're a terrible match. But because she is who she is, she thinks we're great together. And then she makes it so.

Here's an introduction I made at a Jewish National Fund event in 2003, where Monica was honored for her efforts to build a reservoir in Israel:

Hello, everyone. I'm sure Monica and the other honorees this evening join me in welcoming you, and in apologizing for the cash bar.

I just wanted to get in a few words about my wife. This is one of those rare moments where she's not speaking.

Look at all the Jewish people! It's very nice—you should know that we have so many relatives here to see Monica honored tonight. We're thrilled they're all here—they came from Israel and New York and the Holy Land: Atlanta, Georgia. For you gentiles with us this evening, these are Orthodox Jews, who normally don't even recognize those of us who are reformed, or as we're sometimes referred to—lazy.

But they are here for Monica. What does that say about Monica? That not only will she create peace in the Middle East between Jew and Arab with her nondenominational reservoir, she will accomplish an even greater task. She will bridge the gap in the Rosenthal/Auerbach/Hirsch family between the Jews and the people "who will someday get it."

Only Monica can do this. She is good. Truly good. Anyone who meets her, gets that. Anyone who meets her, loves her. This has been a tremendous pain in the neck to me. So many friends! Calling all the time: "Monica—we need you for this. Monica—come with us. Monica—build the temple." Nobody calls me. Unless they want to leave a message: "Just tell Monica we want to name the hospital after her."

I don't blame them. It's hard not to like her.

Twenty years ago, I was living in New York City, near my grandmother Oma, in Washington Heights. She had lived in Washington Heights since after the war. It's where my parents grew up and met each other, and it was nice to live there. Not only were the rents stabilized, I used to go over to Oma's apartment as a starving actor, and leave not as starving. One day I told Oma that I met someone. And before she was happy for me, she asked, "Yah, yah, is she a Yewish girl?" "Well," I said, and that was the end of the conversation. She took the matzo ball soup away from me and went into the kitchen. I got very angry with her. I expected more from her, because she was an extremely bright woman. I suggested that she meet Monica before making up her mind so fast. This was a risky thing for me to do. I really liked that soup. But Oma, who was eighty-something at the time, and had reason to be a little tough on this issue, agreed to a meeting with the non-Yewish, in fact Yirish, "girlfriend." Camp David was booked so we held the meeting in Oma's apartment. I'm not exaggerating—within fifteen minutes Oma and Monica were best friends. Yapping away, laughing, making dates. It was very sweet and wonderful. Two hours went by and I realized, where's my soup? They're girlfriends and everyone could care less about me.

And so it was to be that Monica became the favorite. In the whole family, but especially with Oma. Even when I came out to LA to try it out, Monica stayed in Washington Heights that first year, and did everything with Oma—concerts, museums, movies, dinners. I would call to see how everyone was doing, and they would tell me, "You can stay there a little longer."

But this is the power of Monica. Oma didn't even want to meet her. And ten years later, when Oma died, there was only one other person who was in the room with her holding her hand.

Oma did get one good one in on me though. Back during the time when I was out here without Monica, I got a phone call one day. It was Monica: "I'm converting!" "I don't understand," I said. "You're not doing this for me, right? I mean, I don't care about that stuff and I will not be pressured into marriage." She said, "Don't flatter yourself, it's because of Oma."

Tonight I'd like to reveal to Monica that Oma probably had conversion in mind at the first meeting, she just needed me out of the way first to begin her work. In fact, I think I remember Oma saying to me, "Vy don't you try sings in Cali-for-nia for avile?" (She could run for governor, Oma.) Anyway, I know Oma is watching tonight, so proud of her Yewish Monica, and laughing at me.

I have to sell things all the time—stories, ideas, shows. I never have to sell anyone on Monica. It could be a touchy thing to put your wife in your TV show. People will talk and make the obvious comments. I never worried about it. Just watch, and then talk. I know she's great. And if you've seen the show, you know, too. I love that she's funny. That's the first thing I look for when I'm shopping for a person. Then I found out all the other stuff. The reasons you're all here tonight. I was just a little smarter than you though, because I married her.

Ladies and gentlemen, my beautiful girl, Monica.

I think I'm very nice to have shared that speech with you about how wonderful Monica is. It sounds like it would be a dream to live with her, doesn't it? Here's a story I didn't share at the big fancy Jewish awards dinner. When we first got an apartment in Hollywood, Monica made friends with a very grand old lady upstairs named Joan Blair, and Joan Blair invited her into her apartment, and Monica started to notice pictures on the wall of Joan with the Marx Brothers, when she was young and beautiful. And there was Joan with Orson Welles. "What was this?" asked Monica. "That was *Citizen Kane.* I was the head of a brothel. My scene was cut by the Hayes Office," said Joan Blair, happy to have such interest from a young ingenue. "And this is from *The Shop Around the Corner,*" which Monica had just watched. Joan said, "Yes, I had lines in that one."

And Monica said, "Of course! You say, 'You would know, Mr. Matuschek.'" And Joan Blair said, "Yes, that's me!" And they became instant friends. Now this woman was about eighty-two, and Monica says, "Are you still acting?" "I've been thinking about it," said Joan Blair. "And I'm thinking of getting new head shots." (Because the ones when she was seventy-nine weren't quite cutting it anymore.)

So Monica says, "Great, a project," and she takes Joan for new head shots. They go for the photos, and now it comes time to pick up the head shots. Monica asks, "Joan, do you want to go?" "Yes, let me just gather my things," says Joan Blair, and off they go in the first little car we could afford to the strip mall where Monica's going to pick up the head shots. It's really hot outside on this particular day and Joan says, "I'll just sit in the car." So Monica says, "Okay, but it's so hot today." She leaves the car on so that the woman gets air-conditioning and she runs in to pick up the head shots.

She's at the counter a few moments when she hears *Screech! Crash! Screech!* outside. And then nothing. Monica looks out the store window, and she can see in the distance—there's a van parked across the street sideways, all smashed in. Monica walks outside and she notices glass all over the back of our car, our rear smashed in, and here's Joan Blair, crossing from the driver's side of the car around to the passenger side. Monica looks in the window as Joan puts on her seatbelt and calmly says, "Let's go." Monica says, "We can't go. What happened?" And Joan Blair says, "I thought I saw a better spot."

Joan Blair had gotten behind the wheel, put the car in reverse, driven our car backward across the street, into a van, and then put it in forward and driven back to the spot. I've tried to explain to my wife that no good deed goes unpunished, but she doesn't listen to me. She *loves* people. She truly is the queerest girl in the world.

And so when Amy returned to Robert's life, her presence was very well received on our show, and so was her on-screen family. They were all so terrific that immediately after the table reading of their first appearance together in "Just a Formality" I went over to the phone on the stage, called Les Moonves, and said, "I might have a spin-off for you."

We made Fred's and Georgia's characters (Hank and Pat) religious because we thought they'd bounce off Marie and Frank pretty well, and they did. The first time they met one another was in an episode called "Meeting the Parents" (Lew Schneider and Mike Royce), and suffice it to say they didn't get along too well, they fought over everything, they fought over praying, and no one on either side of the aisle was looking forward to the wedding.

Also as part of this arc of stories, we did Amy's bridal shower, in which Debra has a tiff with Marie, drinks too much, and then falls asleep behind the wheel of her parked car, landing her in jail. This part of the story really happened to writer Leslie Caveny, who spent the night in a cell with a one-armed prostitute, but we didn't put that in because the real life was too jokey for the sitcom. We covered Ray's bachelor party for Robert at Frank's lodge (Mike Royce, Tom Caltabiano, and Ray), where Chris Elliott, as well as Ray's and my real-life fathers, help to ruin it for Robert. My father had a line: "We have balloons, but we can't blow 'em up."

Before we got to the wedding episode, our season finale, we actually needed one more story to complete our order. I asked, not quite kidding, and as usual, if anyone had gotten into a good fight with his wife lately. Tucker Cawley slowly raised his hand. It seems that on our last group trip (we had all gone to San Francisco to see the Rolling Stones), Tucker and his wife, Aileen, had had a suitcase that they brought home, and that Tucker deposited at the foot of their bed. It remained there, unpacked, for a day. And then another day. And then several weeks. Tucker stubbed his toe on it getting into bed one night and muttered under his breath, "Huh. That suitcase is still there." And, as his wife turned the page in her magazine, she replied, "Huh." So although the subject was never formally broached, Tucker thought that perhaps, yes, they were indeed having a fight over whose job it was to move this suitcase. Tom Caltabiano, still the only bachelor among us, thought this was insane. "Just move the suitcase!" he yelled. "Who cares who's supposed to move it?"

And then, as one, the rest of us married guys in The Room seriously pointed at Tucker and said, "You do not touch that suitcase."

We thought it wonderful that after seven years of mining our lives for stories, we could still surprise ourselves with a topic we hadn't hit on yet. What I loved about the story was that the physical subject matter literally was "Baggage." Tucker hit it out of the park. I won't say it was therapeutic for him but while writing such scripts, many times any one of us could be seen making "take that!" faces. The actors were, as usual, tremendous, and this was one of our best episodes.

"Robert's Wedding" capped season seven with a special forty-five-minute episode. Why forty-five minutes? Because that's what the story required. It was more than a half hour, but I couldn't think of enough story for an hour. *CSI Miami* could run long that night. There are a couple of things that came from life here, too. No, my mother did not interrupt our ceremony when told, "Speak now, or forever hold thy peace." But the speech that Raymond makes as best man was based loosely on my own toast years ago at my brother's wedding. Making jokes about the family is where our show had its roots, and so this episode brought the whole thing full circle. We just wanted to make our sweet little point that is the foundation of the show, and of life, in fact: Families don't mean to be terrible, they just are.

And then came Robert and Amy's first dance. People tell us that's one of their favorite moments from the series, and it's one of mine, too. When Monica and I got married, I was somewhat nervous about having to dance in front of people. I always feel that I look like a bird with a hernia. So to distract from this appearance, I thought that rather than dancing soulfully to "Close to You," we should maybe do a funny dance.

We danced to Louis Prima's "Buona Sera," which starts romantically, even nobly, but then, if you know Louis Prima's work, segues into crazy, fast-paced anarchy. Monica is a great, and hilarious, dancer, and my bride and I celebrated our coupledom with lunacy. It's been that way ever since.

It was hysterical to see Brad, a fantastic dancer in his own right, do this turn with Monica. (People ask me what it's like to see my wife with another man. I always say to Brad, "I have to, but you?") Robert and Amy danced to a remix of Elvis's "Little Less Conversation," because we needed the fast pace right away, and that song reflected back thematically on what Marie did at the ceremony. When we shot it that night, as I watched that dance and heard the audience's genuine reaction, I thought: *This moment has everything the experience of doing our show is for me—surprise, inclusiveness, craft, delight, teamwork, spirit, huge laughs, love, celebration, and above all, family.*

The show didn't change much after that, but because of this new development in Robert's life, and because of the infusion of new blood into our stories in the form of Amy's family, we could actually see doing an eighth season. The writers' families obliged us by providing some more material, and the situations that had already been established in the series would also generate a few of their own logical stories. We'd go around for one more ride. One thing bothers me to this day: I never did find a way to use that Joan Blair story. But you can't use everything. Like a one-armed prostitute in jail, some things are just better left in real life. Lew Schneider was on another vacation with his family one winter, and he returned to the ski lodge laden down with the kids' coats, hats, and equipment, and as he was struggling to get on the elevator, he dropped his key ring in the gap between the door and the floor—straight down the elevator shaft. These were his house, car, and office keys, and he, appropriately, flipped out. His wife, Liz, tried to cheer him up. "Look at it this way, honey," she said, sweetly, "at least you could get a story out of it." Lew glared at his bride and snapped, "No, no, we already did the story where Ray loses his wedding ring down the air-conditioning vent, so this isn't a story—this is just something shitty that happened!"

I love that story. Because what it really says is that Lew will continue to pay for the rest of his life for taking me to the "All-Inclusive Resort."

13

Wrap It Up

"Wrap it up" is the only thing you can see if you're fortunate enough to make it to the stage at the Emmy Awards. The audience at home can't see it, but there's a twenty-foot screen placed in the audience, directly in front of you. The moment you reach the microphone it begins flashing: "Wrap it up."

We were not nominated in any category the first two years of *Raymond.* Our third season, we got a few nominations, and that's when the trouble started. By trouble, I mean that "oy vay" feeling that immediately follows the "Hey, we were nominated!" feeling. (Now, I expect no one to feel the least bit sorry for me here—this is simply the tale of a schmo, who, having all his dreams come true and then some, can still find the bad in any situation. It runs in the family. You never want to be *too* comfortable, and I figured out a perfectly good way to be miserable at the Emmy Awards.) For me, it's "oy vay" because of the possibility of having to speak to hundreds of people in the theater, and millions of people in their homes, in their underwear judging what you're wearing. My stomach hurts thinking about this. I automatically go to, *Here's a chance for everyone to see how not funny you really are.* And the nominations are a few months before the awards, so you have more than enough time to get good and crazy. The only way to abate this feeling is to prepare something to say—this way you at least are jumping with a parachute. You want to make sure it's a good parachute, and so you give some thought to what you'll say. And once you do that, you care about it. And once you care about it, you're dead.

When I sit in a theater, in a tuxedo, for three hours, waiting for our category among the other very dressed-up people, I always feel like throwing up. And then . . . here it comes, they might call your name, you might have to get up there. Do you remember what you're going to say? What if I forget? What if I flip out and get to the microphone and say, "I love the Taliban!" It's live television. Anything could happen. You'd better be funny. People will hate you for taking their time and being boring. Deep breaths. Just remember what you prepared. You can do this. "And the winner is . . ." Here we go . . .

"Not you!"

Yes. That's what it feels like. Like you trained for a marathon and you get to the starting gate and the gun goes off and someone says, "Not you." So it's truly the worst of both worlds for a semi-neurotic: worrying about getting, and then not getting. I got to have this feeling in 1998, 1999, 2000, 2001, and 2002. The actors won a few times during those years, deservedly so, and we were always absolutely thrilled for them. But my stomach had been to the dance, and danced around enough, and it had to lie down. Couldn't they just announce the nominees and then have a big luncheon with their five favorite shows, say that everyone's terrific and then we all eat lobster? No, it has to be a horse race or it's not entertaining for the people. And it'll be broadcast live so we can show the losers' faces *as they lose.* Sons of bitches. The whole thing is so stupid and meaningless. And then we won, and now I like them. In 2003, after seven years, Tucker's script for "Baggage" won, and then we all won

Outstanding Comedy Series. We yelled, and hugged, and went up there, on the stage. I got to the mike, looked out, and saw, "Wrap it up, Jew."

I can see the subtext.

I swallowed hard and said, "Very nice. I have to tell you, years ago, when we first started, I got this call from an executive: 'What are you trying to do?' I said, 'What do you mean?' He said, 'I don't get it—what kind of show are you trying to do?' I said, 'Oh. We're trying to do an old-fashioned, traditional, well-made, classic type of sitcom.' And he said, 'All words we should be avoiding.' So I said, 'What words should we be running toward?' And he said, 'Hip and edgy.' So . . . that's what we did. I'd like to thank my down-with-it wife . . . my off-the-hook kids . . . and especially, my parents, Mr. and Mrs. Hip and Edgy Rosenthal."

I thanked the audience for watching and got the hell off the stage. It was a very wonderful evening, full of clinking glasses and celebrating, of congratulations from people we're fans of, but especially because I got to share this, seven years' worth, with my *Raymond* family. That's what the statue is to me most of all: a souvenir of a great night with my friends, and, a horribly pointy weapon to be kept on a high shelf. I heard later that many different executives were wondering if I was referring to them in my speech. Why would they think that . . . especially if they didn't think those things about our show at the time? Hmm. I also heard that I forgot to thank Les Moonves specifically. For which I apologized, and continue to apologize for years later, and in this book, because he, more than anyone, was responsible for our being on the air, and because I have children and enjoy seeing them.

With nowhere to go but down, we went back to work. There was no overriding arc to season eight, but we would have fun exploring Robert and Amy's new marriage against the backdrop of the old marrieds, Ray and Debra, and the old, old marrieds, Frank and Marie. This was one of the main reasons to get Robert married.

The moment Robert and Amy returned from their honeymoon they were given a true Barone welcome in the form of Marie's bothering Amy over the "Thank-You Notes" from the wedding. After much torture, Amy stood up to Marie, saying "I'll get to them when I get to them." As Marie gasped, Debra saw this as the perfect opportunity to enlist Amy on her side, stage a coup, and finally depose the family's dictator. (This was one of the times we could view our show's situation as a parable.) But this coup was not to be. Marie won again, and a proper thank-you note was written. In my family, where a similar situation was the inspiration for this episode, the topic of thank-you notes was apparently such a raw nerve that when this show aired, there was, and still has been, no comment. (I'm just thinking I must be an idiot to bring it up again.)

No episode summed up the three stages of marriage better for us than "Misery Loves Company" (Aaron Shure). Robert and Amy celebrate their three-month anniversary, amid the cynicism and outright hostility of all of Amy's new in-laws. After all the arguing, we felt obliged to tell our audience how we, as writers, really felt about marriage. We wanted to impart real philosophy and wisdom here. What had we, as educated, married writers, learned over the years? Marie says (to both couples): "You don't know what marriage is. Look at us. We've endured. We have been through it all. And now . . ." Frank: "We're waiting for death."

Then Ray makes a toast: "To marriage. Till death do us part." Now I would never say that I feel stuck till the death in my marriage. Certainly not loudly. And speaking for my wedded brothers in The Room, none of them feels this way, either. But I think there are those among us who, when watching this episode with their spouses, stayed very still until the show was over . . . and then, as their wives turned to them, shrugged.

These were the types of programs we wanted to present in this, our last season. The main concern for me was: How to end the series? I knew what I didn't want to do—I didn't want to do the type of last episode in which the series suddenly changes drastically. That never seemed satisfying to me, because whenever a series was closed with something like that I was always frustrated that the characters I loved were inextricably changed forever, and so I had to change how I felt about them forever, or until the bad reunion show. Couldn't we end with a typical episode that, just because it was the finale, would have extra resonance? We entered the lives of these characters in the middle of their story; we could leave them there—nobody moving away, nobody dead. Just do a good episode, and maybe have some reaffirmation of the overall theme we'd tried to hit on occasion.

I had a story idea during season seven and brought it into The Room, where we decided this would be the finale, whenever that would be. So when would that be? I had thought that, our stories bolstered by the new marriage, we could squeeze by with twenty-four more episodes for a season eight. And then, just after the start of season eight, CBS made its opinion clear that we couldn't leave without a season nine. So did the press; so did many letters from viewers; so did our families. In fact, my father, who was a recurring actor on the show, forbade the end of the series, ever. My mother, who has to live with him hanging around the house instead of hanging around our set, was also not pleased.

I talked it over with Ray, who was in agreement with me that we should get out while we were not yet lousy. I gathered the writers in October of this eighth season, and told them about all the reasons all the various factions wanted us to do one more season. Arguments for and against ensued. All of us loved the job, loved one another, loved the annual trips to Vegas, loved the dice games when we should have been working, loved going to the movies when we should have been working, loved the laughing-till-crying runs in The Room, loved the food, loved the free candy and gum—that wasn't the point. The point was what it always was: Where the hell were the stories going to come from? Everything that was now being pitched to and from us was either not so good, or we had done it before, or both. After much discussion, here's what we decided: We owe it to everyone—cast, crew, network, audience, ourselves, my father, my mother—to at least *think* about this decision. We'll reconvene on this subject in January and see if we have any stories for a ninth season. Agreed.

January 2004. We have our story meeting in The Room. For hours, we pitched everything we had all come up with over the last four months for a possible ninth season. Ten very experienced writers, plus ideas from the outside, four months of thinking. After doing the show for eight years, you know how many good stories we had at the end of all that in January? Six.

Six episodes do not a season make, unless you're in England, where sometimes that's the whole series, or you're in America doing the Robert Mitchum sitcom. I did think that whatever number of good stories we had by that day could be doubled in the time we had before another season started. So I called Les Moonves, and told him we could do a twelve-episode season nine. He said, "That's great! We need eighteen episodes." I explained how I didn't think that was possible because it was all about the stories. Les explained that it was really all about the number of reruns he could show in a season. We were each desperately trying to make the other understand the situation. Les said there was absolutely no way, no way on earth, they could take fewer than eighteen episodes. Finally I said, "How about fourteen?" Without missing a beat, Les said, "Seventeen." I said, "Fifteen." He said, "Sixteen." "Done." Season nine would be sixteen episodes long, and then . . . we'd have to go.

We finished season eight with an amazing pair of performances from Ray and Brad. In "Golf For It" (Tom Caltabiano, Tucker Cawley, Mike Royce), Raymond and Robert spend a night in a van, waiting for the public golf course to open. While they do, the subject of conversation turns to who will get Mom when Dad dies. Not usually the stuff of comedy, but with this mom, the brothers decide to golf for who gets her. At first, the argument is over who gets stuck with her. And then they slowly realize that they each want her, and now decide to golf *for* her. Sibling rivalry, fear, jealousy, sadness, jokes, triumph, and a jelly doughnut fight all transpire during an eighteen-page, two-character scene in the front seat of a van. Brad and Ray got every bit of it in the first take, and it was the only time we'd ever seen a standing ovation from our studio audience after a single scene. It was a one-act play, exactly the kind of theatrical event we had always aspired to. It was a joy.

Something odd happened to me during the hiatus between seasons eight and nine: Someone wanted me to become an actor again. Two years earlier, to my surprise, the great writer, producer, and director James L. Brooks (*The Mary Tyler Moore Show, Taxi, The Simpsons, Terms of Endearment, Broadcast News*) had wandered into a seminar on sitcoms I was doing with some other writers and he came backstage afterward. I was stunned to meet him, especially there. Was he bored, and wanted to see people pretend to know what they were talking about? "Hey," he said to me. "Did you ever do any acting, man?" I said, "A long time ago." He said, "Give me your number, I might have something for you." I said, "Don't mess with me, James L. Brooks, because I'll only drop everything to follow you. I'm happy to just have lunch with you."

He called, and we had lunch, and became friends, and had lots of lunches and dinners. Very nice. He never brought up his silly acting offer again, so I forgot about it. Two years went by, and one day he said, "Remember that part I said I might have for you? It's the role of a chef, and you'd be working for Adam Sandler. I need you to read to make sure, but we're friends now so it'd be too weird to have you read for me in person." I didn't know what the hell he was talking about. I was just shocked he, or anyone, wanted me to act. Jim Brooks asked if I could get to the Venice Beach casting offices that day to be put on tape for *Spanglish.* I said, "I can't go to Venice today, I'm running *Raymond.*"

Jim Brooks said, "There must be something we can do."

I asked our wonderful *Raymond* casting director, Lisa Miller Katz, to come into my office. I told her the situation, she looked at me for a few seconds, and then she came back to my office with a camcorder and her assistant, Maggie. I read for them while Lisa read the Adam Sandler part and Maggie filmed. Now, these ladies only knew me as the showrunner for the past eight years. For me to do this in front of them was a little like dancing around naked, singing folk songs. When I was done, I told Lisa to pick the take she liked and send it to Venice. "I'm not going to think about it."

For the next two days this audition was the only thing I thought about. What was I doing? I had a nice life, ran a nice TV show, and I was an actor waiting by the goddamn phone again. The only thing I was thinking was, *Why hasn't Jim Brooks called?* Finally he calls, actually offers me the part, and says, "So, you wanna do this?" I said, "Only since I'm five."

And so at last I was an actor. I had to do quite a bit of research to be halfway believable as a chef. I know a lot about restaurants, I've even invested in a couple because I love them, but I'm no cook. It so happened that the consultant on *Spanglish* was Thomas Keller, arguably the best chef in the country, if not the world. I got to spend some time with him in the kitchen. I observed Keller at his New York restaurant, Per Se, and I worked at the LA restaurants Spago, Grace, and our place, JAR. I had a chef come to my house and cook with me. I made my own ravioli. I had a ball. And then I got to be in a Jim Brooks movie. It was a little part, but you have to remember I couldn't get arrested as an actor in New York, and here I was in a Jim Brooks movie. So now I tell people that this is how you become an actor: very easy. You study your whole life, struggle for ten years, give up acting, become a writer, work on mostly terrible shows till you find a comedian, write a show for him, have it be successful, stay with it nine years, go on a panel and talk about it, have a great director see you there, and get cast by him in his movie.

This actually led to other small roles, like in *The TV Set,* from Jake Kasdan, where I played a network television executive (I had some insight to bring to the role) and *Curb Your Enthusiasm,* where I played poker with Larry David. All fun, all great experiences. And after running a show for nine years, I can tell you that acting is a vacation. I can also tell you that while running our show, I learned a helluva lot from the other side of casting. Advice to my fellow actors: Always memorize your audition, and don't treat it as an audition, treat it as a chance to perform that day. Then, if you don't get it, it's not because you weren't prepared, and you can at least feel good about yourself. And always try to get the first appointment. If you're good, you'll be the one to beat. If you're bad, it wasn't you, it was the idiot doing the casting.

Season nine. We were told that there would be a whirlwind of publicity surrounding our farewell, and we had seen it recently with *Seinfeld, Friends,* and *Frasier* going off the air. A CBS publicist told me that, among other events, *The Oprah Winfrey Show* was going to do an entire episode about us and that I'd be on the show as well. "Really? Me, too?" I was very surprised they wanted the writer. Most shows just want the stars. "Of course they want you, too," said the publicist. "This is to celebrate the nine years of the show." *Wow,* I thought in my naive, incredibly stupid way. Not only am I an actor now, I'm going to be famous, too.

A few weeks later, the cast, the publicist, and I were gathered on the set to go over the scheduling of some of these things. This same publicist said, "Now, when the cast does *Oprah* . . ." and "The cast will stay at this hotel when they do *Oprah*. . . ." I raised my hand. "I'm sorry, am I still doing *Oprah,* too?" And the publicist said, "You? Why would you be on *Oprah*?"

Now, I didn't ask to be on *Oprah.* It never occurred to me before the publicist told me I'd be on *Oprah* that I'd ever be on *Oprah.* What the hell was this? I was confused and a little embarrassed, and I told the publicist so after our meeting. The publicist denied ever saying I'd be on *Oprah.* I went home, annoyed. I spoke to a friend of mine who is a successful screenwriter, and he said, "You're an asshole." "What?" I said. "What did *I* do?" He said, "You can't let them do this to you. You're the creator of the show, and whether we like it or not, the *Oprah* episode on your series is going to be part of the cultural record. You have to be on there, and you don't take no for an answer." He went on and on. And the more he did, the more I thought, *That's right! Why shouldn't I be on* Oprah*? I hate this celebrity-obsessed, tabloid, star-driven culture—enough!* I called my agent. My agent just happens to work at the same agency that represents Oprah Winfrey. This should be easy to remedy. They call Oprah's people (nobody actually talks to Oprah), and they call me back. "Good news," says my agency. "You're invited to come to the *Oprah* show and sit in the audience."

Was this really happening? "Excuse me," I said, trying to keep calm, "with all due respect, I am not going to fly to Chicago to sit in the audience like Uncle Shits His Pants while other people talk about how we made the show." Well, that was a wonderful stand to take, but the agency said there was nothing they could do. This was *Oprah* show policy: A filmmaker could get on once in a while, a book club writer, okay, but no behind-the-scenes television people on the couch with Oprah.

Why the prejudice against TV? Movies are just as lousy. Broadway shows are not so hot lately. What was the last book you truly loved? The last piece of art in a museum that really spoke to you? How many *people* do you really like? All I'm saying is: It's not just TV that stinks. Nothing against him, but if Robert Zemeckis was important enough to accompany Tom Hanks with a clip from *Polar Express,* why shouldn't I be on *Oprah* with *Raymond*? I am not Robert Zemeckis, but I am the Robert Zemeckis of *Raymond.*

I was now as mad about this idiocy as anything ever in my otherwise ridiculously happy and lucky life. At the same time, when I was alone, I was thinking, *What are you doing? Nobody wants to see you on* Oprah, *including Oprah. But what if I could tell my Fruit-of-the-Month story on television? Shut up, you dope, who cares? You know those actors who become unhinged and can only focus on the tiny amount of the world they don't have? You are now one of them. I'm ashamed to be you.* These are the normal, everyday conversations in a head that no amount of affirmation or shock therapy can quiet. I decided to forget about the whole thing and enjoy a sandwich. But the following day I received another call: The *Oprah* show would like to come to the *Raymond* set next week to shoot some behind-the-scenes footage for use on the *Oprah* episode. "Oh, that's interesting," I said. "No." CBS publicity was dumbfounded. No? No to *Oprah*? "The *Oprah* show is allowed to have or not have anyone on their set they like," I said. "Me, too." Why would I let them film on the set? They would just edit the footage any way they liked—the writers would probably be represented like all the adults in the *Charlie Brown* TV specials; off camera, with trombones for voices. "Waa-waa-waa-waa."

No, they could bury me, I didn't have to give them the shovel. Weeks later, I was recounting this tale to another friend of mine who happens to run a studio, when he said, "You want to be on *Oprah*? She's a good friend of mine, I'll call her." "Huh?" I said. My friend called me back later that day and said, "All set, you're on the show." Just like that. CBS, my agency, a call from Raymond's people, no one could get me on the show, but one call from a personal friend to the boss . . . done.

The cast and I went to Chicago. On the way, I started getting very nervous, thinking about what I should say on the show. Maybe, if I got a chance, I could do the Fruit-of-the-Month story. That always worked, and now that I was really going to be on, I should do it, I should stick with the tried and true.

If you've never been to the *Oprah* show, it's part television taping, part religious experience, and two parts shriek-and-jump-around contest. I'm just now starting to get some hearing back. We were back in the greenroom, watching on the monitors (we did not meet

Oprah beforehand), and someone came back, took Ray, clipped a microphone on him, and led him out for the first segment. The crowd went crazy. He did great. During the first commercial, someone came back, took Patty, and she joined Ray for the next segment. Next break, they get Brad. (You see where this is going. . . .) Next, Doris and Peter join them on the couch. I'm pacing backstage, wondering how the hell I let myself care about this, how did I allow myself to get in this position? They yanked my chain and now they're going to dump me. I can't take the rejection. I'm too sensitive. This is why I gave up acting. Next segment, Monica joins them. (Monica gets out there and cries because she's so excited to meet Oprah. Queer.)

There are now two minutes left in the show. They clip a microphone on me and have me wait backstage. The show returns from commercial, and then Oprah chats with the cast for another minute. I'm standing right offstage like a guy waiting for a bus he knows is out of service. Oprah then introduces me. Okay. Now, on the monitor, I've watched as each actor has come out and given Oprah a kiss on the cheek, so I see that's what you do. I approach Ms. Winfrey, and she suddenly does something different for me, she extends her arm straight out to shake my hand. Unfortunately, I had already committed to the lean-in and I had to follow through and kiss her on the cheek. (This part was actually edited out of the broadcast.) I'm a bit nervous as I sit next to Oprah on her couch, but the mostly female audience is so beyond warm and receptive, they would quickly make anyone who sat on that couch feel like a returning victorious warrior, or Robert Zemeckis. Oprah asks me about the pilot, and I figure, great, in the short time I have, I can still do my reliable Fruit-of-the-Month story, get my laughs, and be happy. I start getting into it: "And my mother says, 'Did you know you sent me a box of pears?' " The audience is laughing. This was going to be good. Look where I'd come from, I thought, and where I was now. What a wonderful journey. I'm actually going to really enjoy telling this story here. "I said, 'Ma—' "

Suddenly, from the other end of the couch, Doris Roberts, innocently joining in on the fun, leaps up and says, "I can't talk anymore, there's too much fruit in the house!"

The punchline. She jumped to the punchline. But—but—my story—and Oprah thanks us all for being on, and the show is over.

I was done already. Torpedoed from within. I sat there. I thought about God. I thought God was watching me, listening to me. I could hear God speak to me. And God said, "Did you get what you wanted?"

Is that what I had come to Hollywood fifteen years earlier for—this experience? Did I really have this need? Fifteen years ago, I would've been happy to eat anything other than tuna fish for dinner. Yet this was the stuff of dreams for many people. *Oprah.* It occurred to me that I was a boob. I learned from this little lesson in Hollywood values that I should maybe just concentrate on the work. The work is its own reward. I'd heard that from some guy. Some guy who likes work.

Thank God for the work. We opened our last season the way people thought it might end—with someone moving away. In "The Home" (Jeremy Stevens and Tucker Cawley), it's Frank and Marie, who have found an ideal retirement community, eighty-five minutes away, in New Jersey. Upon hearing the news, Robert celebrates by hoisting Amy all the way up on top of the refrigerator. (We lowered the fridge two inches for this stunt.)

Tucker thought that when Ray attempted to do the same with his wife, he'd not be quite as strong as Robert, and would slam Debra into the front of the fridge instead. Still, it's a happy day, until the reality of Frank and Marie's leaving settles in. Robert and Amy inherit their house (for what Frank and Marie paid for it: $25,000), and yet the boys and their wives are certainly forlorn at the end of this episode. We did not say "to be continued" but just left that episode with the two younger couples sitting in the now incredibly empty living room of their parents.

CBS's promo department was always very good about heeding our wishes that important plot information and jokes not be given away in the ads for any given week's upcoming episode. This was essential to me—you can win the battle (people tune in), but lose the war. (They've seen either what's coming or the best jokes in the promo already, and so the show is not as satisfying to them when they watch it. They may be less inclined to watch again.) We wanted people to think that, perhaps for the rest of the series, Frank and Marie would live elsewhere, and now Robert and Amy lived across the street from Ray and Debra. This premise would last until the very next episode, "Not So Fast," which Mike Royce wrote with me, and which details how the retirement community can't live with Frank and Marie, either. They make Ray and Debra take them back. This little arc wasn't just schmuck bait to us. We did this for a reason: to worsen Robert's life. We always felt obliged to give to Robert with one hand and then take back with the other hand, and maybe two or three more hands, also taking. He and Amy, having already given up their apartment for this house, would now have to share it with Frank and Marie. A little more conflict never hurt anybody (on television).

For episode number two hundred, we wanted to learn something we hadn't yet known about the characters. "Boys' Therapy" was about Ray and Frank being forced by their spouses to accompany Robert to his therapy session for the good of their relationships. We had done a show, "Counseling" (Mike Royce), in which Ray and Debra went to a marriage counselor, and this had been based on several of our experiences. Aaron Shure has said that the reason he went with his wife to counseling was because "it was the closest I'd ever get to a threesome." I still had a few more things to say about therapy. I wouldn't call myself an expert, but I've dabbled. Frank pretty much sums up how he feels about therapy in a gesture that Ray came up with for this episode; he tilts his head toward Robert, giving him the finger in his mind. The wives prevail, of course, and the boys must go to therapy together.

Once outside Dr. Greenberg's door, however, Frank balks and steers his sons to the racetrack instead. They win and have a good time, so now they just have to make up what they discussed in therapy to their wives, and they can go to the track every week. It is in the making up of their therapy sessions at the track that they actually have therapy, revealing hidden truths, such as Frank's having been hit regularly by his father as a child. His sons are surprised by this and realize that Frank never hit them. He didn't want to be like his dad. These revelations bring the boys closer together with their father. Talking your issues out, whether with a doctor, or with your dad at the track, works. Unfortunately, the girls read in the obituary column that Dr. Greenberg has died this past week, and the boys come home and continue to boast about what great progress they made in their session today with the good doctor. They then have their heads handed to them.

And Robert, who now needs to talk to Dr. Greenberg about these troubles, can't. The tag of this show involves Marie, following through on her threat to bring her psychoanalyzing cousin Bella to the house for some intensive therapy with her horrible husband. During the filming, between takes, our script coordinator, Steve "The Hawk" Meyer, thought of a perfect moment to end this episode: Cousin Bella details her plan for how Frank should "really listen" to his wife from now on, and then asks Frank what he thinks. Frank just tilts his head toward her.

"Pat's Secret" (Tucker Cawley) revealed our beloved Pat (Georgia Engel) to be a smoker. When a character is so defined, and so well played, just that simple idea would be enough for us to see the potential for a full story. If you watch the episode, I hope you notice the expertise with which Georgia handles her cigarettes and the flick of the wrist with which she dispatches her lighter. Georgia doesn't smoke (of course), but she learned everything she needed to, just for this episode, to become a derelict. As a person, Georgia is every bit as sweet and wonderful as her character, but she is a consummate professional, and a brilliant comedian. Again, every actor on the show was so fantastic, there were times I couldn't believe our luck that they were all in the same place.

And then it was time for the idea we had kept in the drawer for a couple of years to come out. I had written the story, but I wanted to write the script with everyone in The Room. It's how we wrote many episodes, and that's how we did "Finale." We had a bit of a struggle with the Writers' Guild, but in the end the credit for this episode would read "Written by Philip Rosenthal, Ray Romano, Tucker Cawley, Lew Schneider, Steve Skrovan, Jeremy Stevens, Mike Royce, Aaron Shure, Tom Caltabiano, Leslie Caveny." It was easy to write, we knew what we wanted to say by this point, but I can't say there wasn't a lump in the throat as we were writing the last scene together. This episode ultimately said how we felt about our experience on the show, about one another, and about our audience. And we wanted to tell a good story.

The story involved Raymond's needing to have his adenoids out and being a big baby, not wanting to have the simple operation. Debra, Frank, and Robert all make fun of him—the guys crowd him at his own kitchen table and eat the soup Marie made for him, which she thinks will cure him. As Ray complains that it's getting crowded in here, Robert suggests that he just needs a bigger table. Ray just wants them out of the house—he's a nervous wreck about his operation, so much so that on the day of the event, he makes sure that every adult in his family is in the waiting room while he goes under the knife.

While there, they make fun of him some more, until Marie admonishes them, and leaving for the restroom, demands that they all have proper looks of concern on their faces when she returns. A nurse then comes out from the OR and asks to see Debra. She informs Debra that Ray is having trouble waking up from the anesthesia. Debra gets frightened and calls for Robert. "He's not waking up." Robert starts to get very upset, too—he wants to get into the OR to be with his brother. (Ralph's reaction when Norton got hurt.)

Frank and Amy join them in panic right as the OR doors open and a doctor emerges to tell them all that Ray is awake now, and perfectly fine. We've all had such scares—the guys and I had even shared some of our real-life ones in The Room. Sometimes, of course, they aren't just scares, but real life is hard enough for people. We felt we could make our point without our audience losing its friend and turning this finale into a "Very Special Tragic Episode of the Show You Were Hoping Would Make You Laugh." The Barones' scare lasted thirty seconds. I will say that because it was a finale, we knew the audience might think, *Would they really kill him? They don't need him anymore,* and, we hoped, be at least a little nervous for those seconds, just as Raymond's family was.

When she calms down, Debra gathers the family around her. "Listen, what happened in there," she says, "nobody tells Ray." And Frank adds, "Or his mother." That's the first act.

The second act opens on Ray in bed, happily eating the requisite ice cream, when Debra comes in from shopping for him. She sits next to him on the bed and stares at him wistfully. Ray thinks she's nuts and asks her what's up.

DEBRA

I was thinking . . . nothing, just tomorrow all the stuff I have to do, I was gonna get up and make breakfast, and take the kids to school, then I have to do some grocery shopping, we need chicken and some green beans . . . and cereal . . . and . . . potatoes . . . and shampoo . . . and cookies, then I was gonna pick up the dry cleaning—they still have some of your shirts—then I was gonna get the kids . . . take the boys to soccer . . . they got new uniforms and they look really cute . . . and then I thought maybe you'd meet us at Marco's for dinner, just . . . nothin' special, just get a pizza . . . then come home, put the kids to bed . . . maybe watch a movie?

SHE IS CRYING BY NOW. RAY LOOKS AT HER FOR A MOMENT. SHE SMILES AT HIM THROUGH HER TEARS.

RAY

Time of the month, huh?

Debra's speech was our little nod to the classic, universal play *Our Town,* where Emily realizes that the greatness of life is in everything she took for granted every day. We had the little lump in the throat writing this. And then we had Ray's line, which was us, returning to being idiots.

Meanwhile, across the street, the events of the day have woken up something in Frank, and he is tender to his wife, in an untypical moment. Marie is immediately suspicious. And before long, she gets out of Frank the secret he's hiding from her. She flips out: "My son almost dies, and you don't tell me!?" She runs out the door.

Ray and Debra are starting to enjoy each other's company when Marie bursts through their bedroom door in her red pajamas, and leaps into their bed, literally crawling over Debra to get to her Raymond, to smother him with hugs and kisses. As Raymond screams, Debra says to herself, "I knew one day this would happen."

Soon the entire family is in Ray and Debra's bedroom, and Ray finds out what almost happened to him today. The one thing he wants to know is . . . what did everybody do? Robert lies, saying he was only worried that, with Raymond's nose, it was going to have to be an open casket. Ray is assured that they were all sufficiently worried about him, and they go, leaving him alone with his wife. He smiles at her. "You like me," he says. And this is where I get a little choked up, every time I see it—Debra looks at him. On Patty's face, it's much more than that. Ray gets a little choked up, too, and to me, this is the important part—the show is not just about how much everybody loves Raymond . . . how does *he* feel about everybody? After what he's learned, he can't express in this moment just how much his life with his wife means to him. So he just gestures. He taps his chest and points to her. She knows. He then makes the sign of a heart and points to her. She smiles. He then makes the outline of a much bigger heart, tosses it in the air, and mimes shooting it with a bow and arrow, then sends doves and fireworks and flowers her way. He's a dope, but she reinvites him into bed anyway. "That's right, you were hot for me," he says. "Maybe I didn't wake up." And he picks up where they left off. "Plus, after this, we've got ice cream."

A nice scene. It almost didn't happen.

Rehearsals were going well enough that week, but on Friday morning, as we were going to shoot the episode, Patty Heaton came down with laryngitis so severe she couldn't speak at all—just a whisper would come out. She went to the doctor, got a shot, and the doctor told her not to even try speaking until show time. Tickets for this filming were hard to come by—many fans had traveled from several countries to be with us, and come show time, we went backstage to Patty to see how her voice was. It wasn't. Nothing. She sounded like sandpaper on a cat.

Ray couldn't believe that this faint whisper was all she could muster. "Just talk louder," he said, in obvious denial. We had to cancel an episode filming for the first time in nine years. But we had the rest of the cast come out and take questions from the audience, showed them the pilot, gave them food, and asked them to come back Sunday, when we'd try again. They went home, and we had prepared a little onstage party for the crew and our invited guests, so we went ahead with that.

The big wrap party was scheduled for Sunday anyway, so we would do the show, then go to the big party—it actually was going to work out very well. Except it didn't. Patty's voice did not come back Sunday, and now, not to be outdone, Doris Roberts had lost *her* voice. To top it off, Peter Boyle had come down with a cold.

I think most people would wonder: Was this all real, or psychosomatic? I'm no doctor, but I do know that CBS and HBO had planned a huge party for Sunday night, the venue was paid for, and all the food and decorations were going to go to waste. What to do? We skipped the show and went to the party. Is it hubris to party before the work is done? Possibly, but the food was delicious, and you gotta eat, right? We now scheduled the filming for a whole week after the initial date. That Friday, everyone was in perfect health. We had done a couple of brush-up rehearsals, actually making "Finale" our most rehearsed episode.

What couldn't be rehearsed were our emotions at really being done. Our last scene was the little tag at the end of the show, which had Ray coming down to breakfast with his wife and kids, in a great mood. Frank and Marie barge in, argue over Frank's breaking Marie's stove while trying to fix it, Robert's right behind them, bellowing, "Where am I supposed to eat now?" Amy enters behind him with a cheerful, and queer, "Morning, everybody!" They all squeeze in to eat around the table as Marie takes over the cooking. Debra says to Ray, "Getting a little crowded in here, isn't it?" And Ray says, "We need a bigger table."

As the family argues, makes fun of one another, laughs, and eats, we pull back slowly and fade out the picture, the sounds of this morning lingering a bit longer over final credits.

And then we had a curtain call, and there was the hugging and crying you'd expect. But because the show had been postponed twice, and there had already been two parties, there wasn't much of a party left to be had. It was just us, the cast, staff and crew, our family, and the families of our show on the stage, our stage. We set up a screen and showed the gag reel, and Ray and I each made a little speech, and we just hung out together. It was the best party of all.

Here's a nice insight that helps define show business for me: I went backstage at one point to grab a soda from the big fridge at craft services . . . and the fridge was gone. A giant fridge with big sliding doors like you'd find at a convenience store—gone. We had not been wrapped for an hour before someone came and took the fridge, the craft service table that lived there for nine years, the coffeemakers, the shelves of food, all the things that made life worth living. I found Larry, our brilliant craft service person, and said, "I was just going to get a soda, what happened?" He shrugged and said, "They needed the stuff for the new show across the alley."

14

So What Else Is New?

I didn't really cry that night, not even over the missing food table—the work was a good distraction. I was so busy trying to make sure the show came out well, I didn't have time to think that this night would be the last time working with all these people. Besides, I had no intention of saying good-bye to my friends. It truly was time for the show to end, but that didn't mean my relationships had to. We still have movie nights most Sundays at my house, and my best friends—the writers—and I have a traveling show that I love doing with them. It's called *Inside the Writers' Room.* I got the idea from watching a show with Sid Caesar's writers, and they were all hysterical, recounting tales of working on *Your Show of Shows.* I thought that our guys were funny, too, and that we could make an evening out of telling stories of the horrible things that have happened to us at home, and then show clips of the *Raymond* episodes those stories became.

We first tried this at the Aspen Comedy Festival a few years ago, and it worked so well that a booking agent signed us up, and now we do about a show a month, coming soon to a theater near you. I love that people are seeing and listening to writers, and I still love getting laughs onstage. But the best part is traveling, eating, and laughing with my buddies. I plan on working with all of them in a room again, but until we can, we have this way of staying together and watching Lew act like a monkey.

As for the cast, there was some more publicity to do before the finale was to air in May 2005, more than four months after we had shot it. We were invited to New York (me, too) to do *Inside the Actors Studio* with Sir James Lipton. (He's not really a sir, but he speaks like one.) We taped this in May, the night before the finale was to air, and as we were heading to the stage, I said to Mr. Lipton, "This is really nice that we could all do this together, thank you." And he stopped, looked deeply into my eyes, and said, "It's fucking history, man." Just when you think that you might take yourself too seriously, here comes someone who takes you and himself even more seriously.

First of all, it's a four-hour taping *without a break.* Yes. All six cast members onstage, and me. It was two hours before Mr. Lipton even got to me. I was ready this time, however. I had spoken to Doris backstage. In case I'd get to do my Fruit-of-the-Month story again, I had an idea of how to fail-safe it. "Doris," I said, "I'd like you to do the punchline of the Fruit-of-the-Month story tonight." She was game. My idea was that I'd tell the whole story and when I got to the appropriate place at the end of the story, I'd cue Doris and she could do the last line. Everyone wins. The cue is "And my mom says . . ." Doris had it. "And my mom says . . ." "Right," I said. "And then you say your line." Perfect. Onstage, when Mr. Lipton got to me, one of the first things he asked me about was the Fruit-of-the-Month scene in the pilot. Excellent. "Well," I say, shifting and settling into a comfortable position in my director's chair, "I had sent my parents Fruit-of-the-Month, and I got this call from my mother—"

"I can't talk anymore, there's too much fruit in the house!" yells Doris. Even sooner than on *Oprah.* Genius that I am, I had made her cue line almost identical to one of the first lines in the story. I've decided that I will never tell the fruit story again. Unless someone asks me. And we're alone.

During the evening, Mr. Lipton mentioned many of the distinguished alumni who had sat in those chairs, such as Martin Scorsese, Robert De Niro, Gene Hackman, Jennifer Lopez. Finally, Brad Garrett cut him off, shouting, "All right, we get it! You know some people! You want to impress these kids, name someone they never heard of." Later, in hour four, I was becoming a little punch-drunk, too. I was suddenly feeling like that wild rebel kid in Hebrew school again. When Ray answered one of the questions from Bernard Pivot's apparently famous French television show, *Huer Fleurfleurfleur* (that's not the name of the show, just how it sounds to me), Mr. Lipton told us that Raymond's answer "was very similar to the answer I gave to that same question . . . when I was Bernard Pivot's final guest on *Heur Fleurfleurfleur,* when, for three and a half hours, all of France stood still."

We stood still, too. When he got to me, with the question, "What noise or sound do you hate?" I responded, "Bernard Pivot."

"Excuse me?" said Mr. Lipton. "Bernard Pivot," I said. "Isn't he the one who made up this facachta questionnaire?" "Well," said Mr. Lipton. "If you're not going to take it seriously . . . this questionnaire was created by Marcel Proust." "Oh, no, no, I'm sorry," I said. "This is what we do, we make jokes, I didn't mean anything. Please, I'm sorry. Give me another one." And Mr. Lipton went to the next card and asked, "When you arrive in Heaven, what would you like God to say to you?" I said, "You can go back, but send up James Lipton."

This was all, understandably, edited out of the broadcast. Mr. Lipton was very, very nice to us, and I certainly apologize for the

Hebrew schoolboy maturity, but after four hours, even Vanessa Redgrave probably had to let loose a little.

The following day was filled with more publicity than any of us on the show had ever done. *The Early Show, Regis and Kelly, CNN, The View,* several more, and then media tours, where a phalanx of cameras—dozens of TV shows from around the country set up, one after the other, at a hotel and ask the same questions of the cast about what it's like to be ending. We had never been on the covers of magazines or on talk shows the way, say, *Desperate Housewives* or *Sex and the City* dominated the newsstands and the airwaves. We were seen as the family show, skewing a bit older than the sexy demos the media seems to enjoy so. But now, now that we were leaving, we were the center of attention. So when I was asked what it was like to be ending, the first thing that came to mind was that it was nice how the media gathers around to embrace a death. Also on the schedule for our victory lap that day was ringing the closing bell with Les Moonves at the New York Stock Exchange. That sounded cool, but I can't say I ever had an interest in that kind of thing—I saw scenes of the place depicted in movies, and thought I got it. When we arrived, the cast and I were taken to a large meeting room and given a brief history of the exchange, and told where we'd go to ring the bell. We had a little time to kill, and the president of the exchange asked if we'd like to go on the floor to get a sense of how the place worked. Fine. I knew what this would be like—men running around yelling orders.

The cast and I went downstairs, the doors to the trading floor opened, and we were greeted by hundreds of men and women cheering. They were not working. They had obviously stopped because they heard the *Raymond* cast was coming down. The cheering was shocking, overwhelming. And as we began to make our way across the floor, men and women were hugging us, taking pictures with their cell phones, getting autographs, shouting in their beautiful New York accents, "We love you guys!" The sea of people parted to let us through, but no one was working—they were excited to see their friends.

I expected an army of drones going about their business, barely noticing the Hollywood types walking by, but this was like a Frank Capra movie—so much good will, so much excitement, so much affection: "You make my life better!" We all were teary-eyed, and a couple of them even stopped me—"I know what you do!" yelled one well-informed fan. I can't overstate how huge the reaction was to the cast coming through there—it was like being with the Beatles, and I was Brian Epstein. When we got to the balcony and joined Les, the crowd below cheered and cheered as Les rang the bell and we waved good-bye. The last thing in the world you thought about in this place at that moment was money. We had one more stop to make at a CBS affiliates party at the Museum of Television and Radio, and then we went back to our hotel, changed into comfortable clothes, and joined the writers, actors, and our families for one last party. The hotel had set up a buffet in a meeting room, and adjoining that was a big-screen TV with sofas for us to watch the documentary special on our show and the finale. I sat on a couch with my parents, rightfully, and it was moving to be sitting with them—the cause of a lot of this—and the kvelling was almost too much.

When it was over, we hung out, had amazing chocolate desserts (because if it's not chocolate, it's not dessert), and that's when I became a weepy mess. Again, not so much because it was over, but because we had all shared this wonderful experience and success together, and we started hugging, and if you hug me and cry, I probably will, too. Brad's hugging and crying was the last straw. I almost drowned.

"What are you going to do now?" asked my parents, before we had even left the dessert table. "What's next?" ask my parents and all their friends whenever I see them, or speak to them on the phone. "So what's new?" No matter what has just happened, winning an award, ending nine years of a television show, working with the president of the United States, I still get, "So what else is new?"

Well, I've always enjoyed movies, so I'm taking a meeting here and there, to write, with an eye toward directing. My agency is even starting to send me out on acting roles. And another TV series is not out of the question. But first, I'd like to lie down. You can't run a marathon and then get up the next day and run another marathon. The truth is, I'm busier now than I ever was on the show, and I guess I'm comfortable that way. You just don't want to get too comfortable. What makes me relax is the knowledge that none of these meetings about big important projects will ever work out.

A few months went by, and then in September 2005, we got to go to the Emmys one last time. I wasn't nervous at all, because I was sure we were going to lose to the show of the moment, *Desperate Housewives.* And then we won. Utter shock was the reaction. I stood up in a daze; Monica, still seated, looked up at me, mouth hanging open. "Um, I guess we go up there," I said to her. "Me, too?" she asked. "Yes, you're in the show," I said. She didn't move. "Okay, if you're not going, you have to let me through," I said, as the music was playing and the signs were already flashing "WRAP IT UP." We finally got up there, and I had truly prepared nothing, so I used something I had said a few times during the year. "People have asked me, now that our show is going off the air, if this means the end of the sitcom. I want to say . . . yes. Not only that, but I believe it's the end of laughing. And soon, the end of smiling." I then thanked the audience for nine wonderful years, and got the hell out of there. I got off the stage, and was almost immediately reminded that I didn't thank Les Moonves. Again.

Les, I know you have many more important things to read, but maybe someone who brings you coffee will tell you to turn to this page: We owe the life of the show to you. I thank you for sticking with us, and with me personally. Can I have my kids back now, please?

I also want to thank you, nice reader, for sticking with me during this book, and if you watched our show, thanks for that, too.

How do I really feel about the future of television? It's all cyclical, and all these reality shows will start dropping off, and then the next sitcom hit will come along, and then they'll say, "Wait a minute! The hit is over here now! Run over there and start imitating that!"

Things need time to grow. By the way, about reality shows, why are they so popular now, at the expense of comedies? Because a lot of comedies are not writing real people. The characters are not believable as people. So we turn on a reality show and we say, "That character is funny!" That's a real person that we recognize and relate to, because we understand what it's like to be a real person. So when we watch a sitcom and the characters speak like nothing on the planet, and don't act human, and they're cardboard cutouts of human beings, I'd rather watch the reality show. Even though it's not reality, the people on them remind me of people. We know this, don't we? Even if we don't know it and can't articulate it all the time, we know it intrinsically. "Why am I not relating to this?" Because this is not dialogue that anyone would say, this is not a situation that anyone could believably be in. And here's a person in a reality show that's plopped in the middle of an island, and he's acting more like a person I'm in the office with than this person on a sitcom who is *actually in an office setting.*

We're looking to connect. That's all we do as human beings on the planet—look to connect with other human beings. So we look for the most relatable, connectable thing. Subconsciously, not even consciously. Look at how well documentaries are doing lately. People say, "I love a documentary." Why, because they're so intellectual?

They must see a factual thing? No, because those people, and places, and even penguins in those stories are more interesting to us and more connectable and relatable to us than the crappy supposed Best Pictures that we have to sit through. Where's *Mary Poppins*?

Okay, my wife just told me to stop yelling.

So. What have we learned? It comes down to three things.

1. Be nice.
2. There's nothing wrong with our television, or even the four-camera sitcom. It's a marvelous, wondrous art form (perfectly "in between" theater and film) that has been, and will be again, used for good. Not every show has to be relatable (but maybe there can be a few), not every show has to have topical jokes, not every show has to be for twelve-year-old boys.
3. If you get a job in this art form, and aren't careful, you will get fat. When I hit forty, my doctor told me my cholesterol was somewhat high for my age. I had fooled myself into thinking that if I just ate junk on special occasions I'd be okay. Well, it turned out every day in show business was a special occasion. I was even eating a piece of office birthday cake when my doctor called with my results. He said, "Put the fork down." I did, and like a nervous ethnic person, I overreacted. I did a ton of research to lower cholesterol. Turns out that the same thing you do to lower cholesterol is the same thing you do to lose weight. In a nutshell (this might be the only useful part of this whole book), you cut back on red meat, dairy, and simple carbs (like white flour and sugar). I work out most days, eat healthy most days; I've lost thirty pounds and kept it off. And now I really do eat whatever I want on special occasions. So, pick your spots, and enjoy your

life. Or don't listen to me, get fat, and die young. Maybe that's a good book title.

I want to leave you with what I said to the cast, staff, and crew that night we finally wrapped the show, and it was just us. To you I say, Thanks again for the good life, and I wish for you what I've had—the joy of doing what you love with people you love.

I've been having trouble sleeping lately, and it's not because the show is ending after nine years, or because I won't be seeing most of you on at least a weekly basis for a while—it's because I know that I will probably never work again.

"What?" you say. "Phil? Of course you'll work again, you're somewhat talented, and we hear you may have some of those tribal connections." Tonight I will tell you that part of that is true. But I'm worried that talent doesn't mean what it did when we first sold our little wooden show lo these many moons ago. Talent today means what Paris Hilton does. And my wife will tell you I've never been any good at that. She's an actress, my wife, TV's Amy. And I love her. She's a good first lady. And she's going to be seeing me in a new light very soon. The light of the television in the middle of the day, with my pants off, a bottle of scotch and a bag of chocolate-covered pork rinds in my lap, watching *Raymond* reruns, going, "Hold." But they won't hold. And I'll get mad. Then I'll be telling the kids to hold and they'll cry because Daddy's yelling, so I'll wander out in the street and see the mailman force my issue of *Musical Comedy Monthly* through the slot and bend the cover and I'll say, "Hold!" And he won't know what "hold" means. So I'll beat him with my scotch bottle while my kids look on and Monica films it and sends it in to Fox and they'll order thirteen episodes and that is how I will stay in show business.

So don't be sad. Seriously, don't be sad tonight. I'm going to tell you your future. Let's start with the actors. As much adulation and awards and money and attention as they have gotten, it has not been enough, and they will be the first people to tell you that.

Ray Romano will be a movie star. He will star in a movie about a guy who bothers all his most trusted friends and colleagues about what movie he should do, and they tell him over and over and then he does the opposite and then cries to those same people about it. It will be called *Million Dollar Baby.* And it will be a big hit. In Pakistan—where they won't know till it's too late, this isn't the Clint Eastwood movie.

Patty Heaton will do for shopping in grocery stores what her friend George Bush's flight suit did for him—make turkey look sexy.

Brad Garrett's next job will not come until next Christmas, but he will bring much joy to everyone who visits Rockefeller Center as they gather round his bright and colorfully lit genitalia.

Doris Roberts will become a United States ambassador. To Pakistan. Her first official duty will be to assist moviegoers who want their eyes poked out. And Peter Boyle will star on Broadway in a spectacular new production entitled *Line?*

I did not mean for this to become a roast, it's just my way of dealing with the separation from those that I love so I don't cry. Rory Rosegarten. Hopefully your future will include returning some of our props. For example, I know that Doris wants the big vagina. I just think she should stop saying that out loud to people.

The writers. I love the writers—most of whom have been with us from the beginning and who will now get jobs as men's room attendants, except for Lew, who has had that job before but has been banned from it because he could not resist what the union calls "handling the merchandise."

As for the rest of you—you're coming with me. Whatever I do next, I want you all with me. I hope you enjoy sleeping. And scotch. And me on you.

I have loved these days. I am the luckiest guy in the world to have been thrown together with you—your smiles and laughs and goodwill have made me feel like I wasn't picked last in gym class, and called spaz, and hopeless, and Auntie Mame, and then punched by girls. . . . And I've been carried up by you to a place of wonderful success—not monetary success, although that's very nice, but the truth is . . . I would've done this for free. I'm talking about the more important kind of success: good work, good friends, good food.

We are eternally grateful to our godfather, Les Moonves, who (somewhere) just said, "He would've done this for free?"

Let's thank our families, especially our parents—I can honestly say about mine and Ray's that none of us would be here tonight without them. To Mom, Dad, Mr. and Mrs. Romano, thanks for being maniacs.

I'd like to say something to my friend Raymond. When we first met, I liked you right away, and I got the feeling . . . you didn't quite trust me. I couldn't blame you, I didn't quite trust me, either. But in trying to get that trust, in working with you for ten years, I learned so much from you about being creatively honest and true to yourself, believability, relatability—these are the qualities you brought, not only to your beautiful performances, but to The Writers' Room, to me. You made me better. You all, every one of you, working with you made me better at this job I love. And you made my life better.

Thanks.

We, together, have hopefully made something of lasting

value, something rare in the culture, a work of popular entertainment that looks like it might endure beyond the half hour a week it's been presented. I hope you'll take pride in what we've done and know that you each have been an integral part of our show. We're lucky because we have had brilliant, indelible actors out front, representing us, and I'm including the Sweeten kids and every guest actor we've ever had. And in the engine room, and this is not an exaggeration, the best sitcom writers in the world—most of whom were with us from day one. But thirty years from now, you might see a rerun with the grandkids on their rocket ship or wristwatch, and remember the prop, like the canister (or a big "you know"), or Brad's curly eighties wig in "How They Met," or Frank and Marie's kitchen set, or the Kubrick camera angle in "The Toaster," or the seamless edits in "Dancing with Debra," or the light on the faces when Peter wiped away Doris's cold cream, or the music in the Italy show, or the sound effects of those old "Jazz Records," or the jiggle of the tofu turkey, or Robert's pants that came up to Amy's neckline, or how much the car-through-the-house bit cost, and know . . . you did that. You are why your grandkids are still watching. All of us made a show. We connected. That was the goal. Connect to people. And we get letters from people who say what we do actually makes a difference in their lives, makes them laugh, and that connects us to a big part of the world. Almost every day, almost everywhere, almost every place on earth. We get letters from India, and Scotland, and Sri Lanka: "That's my mother."

So don't be sad. Nine years. We spent a huge chunk of our lives together. I feel like I took a nine-year break from my life and I now go back to whatever that is . . . as a graduate. So don't be sad. Just like school, it's not the end of the most important part of what we've done—become friends. Become a family. What a time we've had. We have accomplished a wonderful thing together, and we are better at what we do now than when we started. We have love, and laughs, and food, and each other and I thank each and every one of you for the gift of getting to be with you. I love you, my dear, funny friends. Let's stay connected. ■